For starters, thanks a n
people who volunteered   ...e
book to see if I'd made a, y ,umb mistakes
and to make helpful suggestions:

From the Speech and Drama World:

Lynne Collinson, Editor of *Word Matters*, the Journal of The Society of Teachers of Speech and Drama and teacher of Public Speaking

Coral Dickinson, Lamda Tutor and Creative Director of Stages School of Acting, Bromsgrove and south Birmingham www.stagesdrama.co.uk

Jules Martin, LAMDA Teacher, Essex, East London
www.lamdateacher.co.uk

Kaz Luckins, Actress, Singer, Fight Director and Drama Practitioner

www.kazluckins.co.uk

And from the Real World:

Rachel Akers

James Friend

Simon Hingley

And a big thanks to Nithil Kennedy who did the drawings on the cover and also the intercostal diaphragmatic breathing diagram.

And I must also say thanks to my own students for being so great to work with and for taking the trouble to provide the hilarious images scattered through the book.

Contents

Introduction

Some people can just give a great speech without even thinking about it, they just walk up on the stage and they give a brilliant speech; no rehearsal, no pre-thought, nothing, they're just brilliant.

I don't know if you've ever met that kid at school who says they never do any revision for exams, and they get a fantastic result, they get one of the highest marks in the class. And they say, " No idea how I did that. I didn't do any revision at all."

Guess what? They're almost certainly telling you a big massive fat fib.

Of course it helps if you're naturally brilliant, but no matter how smart you are, your results will be loads better if you prepare thoroughly. And you want to be good, don't you? You want to nail this speech and kill it. Dead.

Your teacher, if s/he's got any sense, would've given you a fair amount of time to get yourself ready.

So take your time and do it right.

It's going to make you a lot less nervous because you know what you're doing. Anyone who knows what they're doing is less scared than someone who has no flipping idea.

When your teacher tells you you've got to make a speech, give a presentation or a talk, it can make you nervous.

Strange!

Why should you be nervous in front of all these kids you hang out with, why is this any different from just talking to them?

The thing is, it makes pretty much *everybody* scared until they get used to it, until they know how - and then they really enjoy it.

It's true. Really.

I've written this book to show you how to become that person, that person who always looks so confident when they give a talk, who knows how to put the words together in a way that really has an impact, the person who gets a round of applause at the end.

The person you're a teeny bit jealous of.

I've been a Speech and Drama teacher since the day after the dinosaurs uttered their last breaths on Earth, so I know all about it.

I've been an examiner for Lamda, for the London Academy of Music and Dramatic Art and for New Era Academy, so I know what goes through the examiners' minds. (If you're the kind of person who likes to take exams in speech and drama, this matters - if you're not, it shows you how smart I think I am.)

And you know what the examiners really like?

A student who gives a polished performance.

The kind of person who walks into the room with a bright and cheery smile, introduces themselves and then gives a speech that's really well structured and has great detail, is presented confidently with a nice variety of tone, appropriate gesture and movement.

It could be you.

Chapter One

What's Special about Public Speaking?

What is it about making a speech that makes you nervous?

Why should it be such a big deal?

Why is it different from other forms of communication?

Why are repeated rhetorical questions annoying?

In the rest of this chapter, I'll be writing about the reasons why public speaking makes you nervous.

Now if you don't care *why,* you just want to know *how* to do a great speech, then you can skip this bit and go on to Chapter Two.

You're welcome.

Right, for those of you who are still with me, this is why.

It's really because of the live nature of the event and also because of the expectations of the speaker.

You have been asked to speak on stage or to stand in front of a class full of people to give a presentation.

Your audience expects something more special than a written exercise; otherwise why is it a presentation?

The fact that they're expecting something good is worrying. What if you can't deliver?

Maybe your teacher hasn't had the time to give you any special coaching in how to make a presentation (Although if they told you to get this book, give them a pat on the back. Metaphorically - you don't want to get sued.)

They are putting you in the spotlight, 30 pairs of eyes all looking at you.

We need to understand the differences between this type of communication and other forms.

To begin with, **it's different from a document** in that people on the receiving end of your words of wisdom don't have the opportunity to check or look things up online if they don't understand something.

And if they fail to understand the point, they may lose the flow and they may give up listening to you.

It's usually pretty obvious when your audience has stopped listening to you, everyone gets a sense of it; there is a shuffling of feet, there is a fidgeting in seats, there is a surreptitious sneaky looking at mobile phones.

You, as a speaker, become aware of this and it's embarrassing.

If just two or three people in a private conversation witness you making a bit of a fool of yourself, well, it's only two or three people.

 But if you are delivering a speech to lots of people, well, that's a lot of people who have seen you embarrassed, so there is a magnifying effect.

Now think about **a conversation**; a couple of people chatting. The dynamics here are very different: in this context everyone is expected to participate in the conversation, everyone has to take a turn. If one person in the group doesn't take part - is silent - people ask why.

In your public speaking context, this isn't the case. The audience is not expected to take part or say anything. Therefore they may decide not to listen, safe in the knowledge that they are not going to be asked to comment.

So this adds to the pressure on the speaker and it explains why she needs to be entertaining in the broadest sense of the word.

And public speaking is **not like recording a YouTube video**. Because it's live. You can shape your YouTube video; if you don't like it you can edit it, you can delete it, you can change bits. You can pretty much make sure that you don't make a fool of yourself.

Not so in the live event.

But it's not all doom and gloom. The very things that make it challenging can be flipped and make it exhilarating.

As mentioned, if you make a bit of a fool of yourself in front of a small number, it's bad, in front of a large number it's worse.

But just think about this: if you say something that entertains a couple of people at school, you feel good; if you entertain a couple of hundred people from the stage, it feels fantastic.

The boost that your reputation and self confidence get from making a great speech is tremendous. It's your opportunity to show off and make a great impression with the effect being magnified by the numbers of people in the audience.

So my objective in writing this book is to help you become a good public speaker. I'm aiming this book at you, a student at school or university, someone who has a whole career ahead of them.

At many points during your life you will be asked to stand up and give a presentation. It might be in front of your classmates in a few weeks time; maybe it will be a presentation in order to get a job in a few years time; it could be at a wedding, heck it could be when you are prime minister.

I want you to be ready. I want you to have a tool kit that you can turn to at any time.

This will be your tool kit.

I rather like the metaphor that I've chosen to use in the title of the book and the image of me, drawn by my former student, Nithil Kennedy. Well, you know, like many of my cars, metaphors always break down eventually. So I'm not going to bang on about *tool boxes* and *nailing* public speaking too much.

But what I will say is this: this book will give you all the tools (probably the last time I will use that word in this context) you will need. Each chapter contains a different aspect of speaking in public and at the end of most chapters is a series of exercises on what you have just read.

You could just idly think about the exercises, or you could write your answers down, you could write brief notes on them and then perform them, or any combination of the above.

The decision is yours.

How to be a great public speaker, if not quite a god.

In the mid 1960s, which I do remember, thanks for mentioning it, when graffiti became a notable and distinguishing feature of urban scenery, one slogan gained a lot of traction, it was found all over the place in cities from London to Johannesburg to New York.

Clapton is God

Eric Clapton, I should say for the youngsters, was, and indeed is, a fantastic rock guitar player. Check him out on Spotify or your young person's equivalent.

Now Eric Clapton himself denied that he had divine qualities, but there was no doubt that he was very, very good with the guitar and one very keen fan - or possibly one very cynical music promoter - had found a way to make this phrase do the 1960s version of going viral.

Obviously, it meant that he was a good guitar player, in fact the best, according to the anonymous graffiti artist(s). Later he said that he found it embarrassing and that he wasn't the best guitarist in the world.

But clearly a lot of people thought he was amazingly talented. And loved his music.

He was able to become so gifted because he loved playing the guitar and he practised. A lot. He knew every note of every song and he knew exactly what everyone else in the band would be doing at any given moment.

Did this mean that his work came across as rehearsed, as lacking in spontaneity?

No, my friend, it made it sound fresh, vibrant and godlike. Ironic, huh.

This utter devotion to, and complete awareness of, the technical aspects of the work and the direction of the concert meant that he actually was free to improvise occasionally.

From competence comes confidence

I'm assuming you know where we're going with this.

I'm coming round to talking about the value of preparation as a public speaker.

<u>Learn the methods, practise them, prepare your piece carefully, rehearse it until it's second nature.</u>

There won't be graffiti saying,

(your name here) is god

But maybe, who knows, you might get:

(your name) is actually very ,very good

Chapter Two

Speech Types

The first thing to do is to categorise.

Now ALL speeches need to be engaging from start to finish. Doesn't matter what category they come into.

But your choice of vocabulary, style of delivery and many other things will depend partly on speech category. Decide what kind of speech you're giving.

Is it -

Persuasive, informative, entertaining, or is it, horror of horrors, an impromptu speech?

Often your speech will be a mixture of these, but usually one of them is dominant;

make sure you have a clear idea of where the balance lies.

Persuasive Speech

This is obviously a biased or subjective speech and the more strongly you hold your opinion, the more forceful and effective your speech will generally be.

The first point you make must be the strongest one in favour of your argument. The body or main section of this kind of speech may be divided into three or four key points.

So the first main point is the strongest one, then we go down in decreasing importance to the second, third and fourth points, where the last one may be something a little bit humorous or possibly quirky.

If you think about it, it's pretty obvious that you have to come out with the most important - *from the perspective of the audience, at least* - persuasive reason first.

I mean, take an example:

Let's call this The Maths Homework/Cinema Issue (TMH/CI)

Supposing it was a school night and you wanted to go out to watch a movie. Let's imagine you have three reasons for doing so.

These reasons are:

- *One of the actors in it is really hot*

- *The subject has a link with what you're studying in Geography*

- *You've heard that this director is very good at cinematography*

Now in what order would you place these reasons if you were telling your parents why you were going to the cinema that night instead of doing your maths homework?

Exactly.

And you may not mention the one about the hot actor at all. But If you did, you would say it as if you were just joking.

You could use a different order, of course, but you would be unlikely to be very persuasive.

So just to repeat:

The most important point first, other points follow in decreasing importance and the last one might be a little bit silly - unless it's so silly it would undermine everything that has gone before. In which case forget it.

The final section of the body can be used to demolish the main counter argument to your point of view. The counter argument is what people who may be inclined to disagree with you would say.

You state what the counter argument is and then make clear why it is false.

In the TMH/CI, the key counter argument would be that you have to do your homework. So before they get a chance to say it you say, "Really, this is homework."

While this is an example from life, the same principles apply to a speech.

Here is another way of thinking about how to organise your persuasive arguments:

Whatever you are arguing for may have three characteristics:

- *It should be superior to other options.*

- *It should be easy to implement.*

- *There will be a payoff.*

It's tricky to use this three part trick in the TMH/CI, but it might go something like this:

There's only one chance to see this film before it's moved out of our town, I can do Maths anytime. And Tom said he can take me, so you don't need to bother. And what I learn about Geography will mean I'll probably get a grade A.

That's the way to do it. But have I written it in the correct order?

Let me know. mike@or8.co.uk

And…

There's a whole lot more to writing a persuasive speech. It's called Rhetoric. It's so important in life in general and speeches in particular that right up until and beyond Shakespeare's time it was part of every school syllabus.

It's so important that I've given it a chapter all to itself. Don't skip it. If you skip anything, skip the light fandango, but don't skip Rhetoric.

Why they stopped teaching it after Shakespeare's time, by the way, I have no idea. But they did. I suppose they thought they knew then better than I know now. It's possible. But I doubt it.

<u>Informative Speech</u>

Keep at the front of your mind the key points that you really want them to understand and to take away from your informative speech.

An informative speech is obviously objective - unbiased - but that does not mean it is boring. On the contrary, you should try your best to make the material fun. It should be intellectually stimulating and exciting. Think wacky science teacher.

Make sure that everything is backed up by evidence and examples. You probably need to do more research than you would for a persuasive piece. Quote experts on the topic.

Give statistics, show charts and graphs; some people are better at understanding and processing material if they can visualise it.

Another way of helping people to understand something is by using a comparison, whether it's a literal comparison or a metaphor. For example, a friend of mine used to give lectures on the waste disposal industry. He always started his presentation by saying,

In England we throw away so much stuff into landfill sites every day that you could fill Wembley stadium with it! Every day!

As well as being a good hook opening - of which more in a moment - this is a great way of helping people to visualise the scale of the problem.

A good informative speech will often feature interesting, unusual props and dynamic, exciting visual aids. But only if they help to make the subject matter clear, not if they distract.

And you will need to think about different ways of conveying the information: explaining, describing, demonstrating, comparing and contrasting.

An informative speech is one whose goal is to explain or describe facts, truths, and principles in a way that stimulates interest, facilitates understanding, and increases the likelihood of remembering the content.

So some of the qualities it should have: creativity, relevance, and memorability. CRAM.

I remember one student doing a speech on the topic of gravity; when speaking to the audience he told them that actually every object has some kind of gravitational field, meaning that the two students on the front row were actually imperceptibly moving closer and closer to each other.

It did cause them to look around at each other in a new light. Especially the two on the front row.

In another example, one of my students recently did a speech on the very serious topic of knife crime and he started by actually quoting the statistics of this sort of horrible crime in the district in which he and his friends lived.

Making it **relevant to your audience** in this dramatic way is sure to grab their interest.

Yet another student gave a talk on astronomy; he told me that a lot of his colleagues aspired to a flashy lifestyle and so he began his talk by telling them of a star many millions of light years away made entirely of diamonds.

Think, too, about the value of repetition. This is especially important when you have key ideas that you really want your audience to remember, you really want your audience to remember, you really really, absolutely want them to remember!

Don't go too crazy with this, it will get on their nerves, they may want to shout at you "yes,we get the idea, yes we get the idea, yes we…"

As with other categories of speech, you always need to hold the audience's attention but with this genre it can sometimes be more difficult, the material may be rather dry so just don't forget to add a little spice with humour, with the occasional story and with **Mnemonics** and **Acronyms**.

An acronym is when you use the initial letters of a phrase to make an abbreviation of the subject. For example the British broadcasting Corporation became the BBC.

And a mnemonic is a way of encoding information in a shortened form. Like the spectrum is sometimes taught using the phrase:

Richard

Of

York

Gave

Battle

In

Vain

Red, Orange, Green, Blue, Indigo, Violet

And Creativity, relevance and memorability became CRAM, as above.

So I tried to think of a Mnemonic for mnemonics and I came up with this:

MAMMIE

Mnemonics,

Acronyms

Make

Memorising

Ideally

Easy

I know, it's rubbish. But can you do better?

I bet you bet you can do better.

Send it in an email if you do think of one, and I'll put it in the next edition with a credit! If it's worse than mine, I'll bin it.

mike@or8.co.uk

You could think, too, about different learning styles. And address them:

- *feeling- provide concrete, and vivid images, examples, stories..*

- *watching- visual aids*

- *thinking- rhetorical questions, explanations, statistics*

- *doing- encourage your listeners to do something during or after your speech.*

And express the speech in language that is appropriate for your audience's levels of knowledge.

Be less technical than you would be in a document. If they really want to look at the technical details then they could do exactly that – read the document.

Entertaining Speech

The key thing to remember here is that the audience wants to feel that no great demands are being made of them. They just want to relax and enjoy themselves, they want to sit there and listen without a care in the world.

Having said that, there is often something to be gained from **audience interaction.** There is a frisson of excitement when the audience realises they may become a part of the presentation.

And it has the advantage of heightening engagement as people wonder if they may soon be on show in the same way the speaker is. This is fine, it's a great way of bringing focus and livening things up. But just take a little care with audience participation, it can be a double edged sword as you are handing over some control of the speech to the crowd. And you are the one who needs to stay in charge. We don't want a free for all.

Entertainment can mean amusing your audience or it can mean engrossing them in a story, perhaps a dramatic story, or it can mean both.

Let's take a quick look at some of the ingredients of humour and then at narrative techniques.

Humour: there are jokes and there are funny anecdotes.

Let's look at jokes first. What is a joke?

Well it consists of two parts: a set up and a punch line. The set up creates a situation or context. The audience is led to believe that a certain type of outcome is likely to follow. The actual outcome differs dramatically from the expectation and rather ridiculously, but in a way that when you come to look back on it you can see it did make perfect sense.

Here is an example of the set up and the punch line. I apologise now if you think this joke is terrible. I quite like it.

I paid a visit to my great uncle; he is 93 years old and this will be the last time I will see him.

No, he's not ill, he's just really really boring.

So in the first part you get the set up. You created an image in the audience's mind of a poor elderly gentleman and of yourself as a kind young visitor; you added a touch of sadness by saying that it would be the last time; this makes your audience think that the elderly gentleman is about to die and that you feel awful about it.

Then we get the punchline: the reason it will be the last time you will see him is because you don't like his company. It's a teeny bit shocking too and that helps.

Useful tip for joke telling. The risk is that they don't think it's funny, they don't laugh. Now, if they do laugh, you don't want to talk over it, because the audience will stop laughing as soon as you continue talking. Which is a shame. On the other hand, if you pause in a way that makes it obvious you are expecting a mirthful reaction and you don't get one, you look silly. So what you do is pause for just a bat's whisker of a moment and make it look as if you are thinking about what you have just said or what you are about to say next. Then if they don't laugh it's fine but if they do, you extend the pause a bit longer to let them enjoy the moment whilst you bask in the glory.

An anecdote is a story about a person that has an amusing twist. It works well when the anecdote is about the person telling the story. It often involves the central character getting into a sticky situation. The audience feels the discomfort of that character but is generally not terribly anxious because of the amusing context of the story.

So here's one that I have used myself in speeches. What happened is more or less true but when I have told it in a speech I must confess to having used a bit of exaggeration for effect.

When I was a Drama Teacher, I was invited on a course at a very posh independent school in the south of

England. In this school they had a library and within the library was another library, the library which contained valuable historical works. There were about 10 of us, 10 drama teachers.

The head librarian of the school took us into this special library and showed us some of the key works. He made a point of saying that these were very valuable books and we had to wear those special white gloves that they give you when you're looking at a very old book that must not at any cost be damaged.

I had in front of me this Shakespeare First Folio. There were only a few hundred of these books published in 1623, seven years after Shakespeare died. The last one to sell at auction went for about 3 million pounds. For me, this was heaven on Earth as a Drama Teacher. You can imagine. I was touching a Shakespeare First Folio. I leafed through the book and I was very excited.

After talking about the books for a while, the librarian said it was time for a coffee break, "Let's go back into the main room to get coffee and biscuits."

So we did but after a few sips, I decided I wanted to take a couple more looks at the First Folio, so I took my coffee and custard cream with me. I went back into the library and started reading Romeo and Juliet. It suddenly occurred to me that if I spilled my coffee now those Nescafe coffee beans would be forever staining an invaluable piece of literature.

And as I thought about this, the more my hand shook and the more my hand shook the more I thought about it et cetera, until the trembling and the coffee swishing about resulted in a little tiny drop of instant coffee dropping onto the immortal words.

Romeo, Romeo, where(coffee stain) art thou...

Dilemma: Should I shut the book and sneak out and pretend nothing had happened or do I go and own up to the librarian?

Now the outcome of that story has been slightly different in different speeches that I've given and so, yes, dear reader, I admit I did exaggerate a bit, but as I said, it was more or less true. And every time I've told it - maybe three times - it has always held my audience spellbound. I think it's because they could easily imagine themselves getting into a pickle where the consequences could have been disastrous. I mean, where would I get three million quid? I'd have to sell a lot of books.

Another side to this (almost) true story, is that it built up my credentials as a bit of a Shakespeare loving intellectual, whilst apparently displaying my vulnerability and thus making the audience like me. Sneaky, eh?

Impromptu Speech

There may come a time in your life when you are called upon to make a speech even though you have had no time to prepare. Maybe the guy who is supposed to be giving the speech has bailed out and they're asking you out of desperation.

Why else?

Only joking, I'm sure you'd be great. However, you would be nervous.

Probably.

Because this remote possibility is a challenging one, or because they are being mean, some examining boards have put the impromptu speech as a part of the examination. LAMDA has it for Grade 6 and above.

Candidates are given three topics and 15 minutes to prepare; they choose one of them, decide who their imagined audience would be and then they have to give a speech of up to 3 minutes on the topic. Thinking of an **imagined audience** can be difficult. In the past my students have used masses of different ones. The old standby is students in a classroom. We've also used:

- Guests at a wedding

- Footballers at half time (being given a talk by the coach)

- The Dragons in Dragons Den

- A Policy Forming Committee

- Parents at a school Open Day

- A Pressure Group

- Voters at a Hustings Meeting

You should try to be creative in thinking of an audience if you do this for an exam. Remember that **public speaking is any situation in which one person is speaking to a group, usually at a prearranged time and place, and the**

group is not expected to interact. Much. Apart from applauding you and throwing money.

Having varied audiences like this gives an opportunity to vary the style and content of the speech.

Whether you are doing an impromptu speech for an exam or in a real life setting, there are some tactics that you can use to make an impromptu less painful.

The most important thing is to have **a clear structure** to your piece.

Because you haven't had time to plan, there is every chance that you might waffle and that you won't have a strong start and you will have a really weak finish - the piece trails off and you end up saying something a little bit lame like

*I am, and, er, I would like to ,erm, well, that's
it, really...*

So here's the plan: think of the attitude,
stance or view that you or the character you
are representing, has to the topic then, in
your speech:

1.   *Express express the stance or attitude that you
have*

2.   *Tell the story which explains why you have that
view*

3.   *Talk about the future*

So let's take an example:

*You are at an Awards ceremony for a club in the
Birmingham Sunday league and the person who was
supposed to be making a speech to congratulate the player
of the year, has called in sick.*

The chairman of the club, Sid Sidebottom, has asked you to do it. You've got 10 minutes. You know that the player of the year is Danny Dandelion. So you rack your brains a little bit and think about what's the best stance to take on DD.

You decide that it is not just that he is a great footballer, you'll say that he is very dedicated to the club .

So that's Part One of your speech. Talking about the twin qualities of football prowess and dedication.

Part Two is to tell a story demonstrating his dedication. Maybe one year he had a really heavy flu but it was a crucial game and so he turned up and played anyway.

Then you move onto Part Three: to talk about the great future ahead of him and he looks as if he's going to be a really great coach , because you know that he's going to retire in three years.

So there you have your three part structure.

1.   He's Dedicated

2.   Story

3.   Future

You can put the story first if you like, it works just as well and may make a more dynamic start.

Speaking of the start, if you do get chance to make a few notes on a piece of paper, as well as writing your three-part structure, can I suggest that you also write down **the very first sentence** that you're going to speak and **the very last sentence** that you are going to speak and make sure that they are both good.

Then you won't have the embarrassment of an awkward opening or close as above.

May I tell you a little story about **the very first sentence**? Yes, Michael, you may. Thank you.

I went to see a play once. I didn't know anything about the piece. But when the curtain went up, it revealed really great scenery: a medieval castle beautifully created with fabulous background. A character walked on in a fantastic costume and my gosh, did he look splendid. He strutted magisterially for a minute, gazed imperiously at the audience and then...forgot his words.

It was excruciating. I mean, the very first words! A look of concern on his face gradually became a look of terror, he shook a bit and the spear he was carrying trembled. Then he rushed off into the wings - obviously to find a script. A minute later he came back on and said the words,

A mighty spectacle will shortly unfold!

Somehow, we doubted it. I don't remember anything else about that show.

But I do remember what it taught me. Get that first sentence in your head. Front of mind. Right behind the eyebrows.

Political Speech

This is pretty much the same as a persuasive speech with the distinction that it is on a political topic - that is, it's about what the speaker thinks the government's policy on an issue or issues should be.

And there is usually an implication that the speaker is expressing the views of a party, so it's not just his personal opinion.

As political issues are usually contentious and as there is usually a prominent political party with a differing view, the speeches can be **combative** and quite fiery in their attack on the counter argument.

The Vote of Thanks

This is a short speech that follows a long speech!

The longer speech is delivered by an invited guest at a special occasion. As the name suggests, it's thanking the speaker for taking the trouble to show up and talk.

She is told how wonderful it is that she could take the time out of her hectic schedule and is praised for the quality of her speech.

The person delivering the vote of thanks will have been listening attentively and have made some notes, then in their piece, they will refer to a part of the speech they found especially exciting/stimulating/amusing.

Exercises for Speech Types

Persuasive

1.   Imagine that you have to give a speech arguing in favour of school uniform.

●   What would be your three strongest points?

●   What order would they come in?

●   Is there a slightly light-hearted reason you could use as a fourth point?

●   What would be the counter argument and how would you destroy it?

2.   Do the same exercise arguing against school uniform.

3.   Ask yourself the same questions about any or all of the following subjects.

- Murderers should be executed

- Private hospitals should be banned/encouraged.

- Space travel/exploration is a waste of money

- Vegetarians are Morally Superior

Informative

Think of three or more topics that you might give a talk about. You could go for things like astronomy, coastal erosion, the voting system, a breed of dog that you like, how to make or cook something. Or think of your own topic, maybe something you would actually like to make a presentation about.

- For each topic find three visual aids. One should be a picture, one should be a chart, one should be in words. For each one, explain how it would help the presentation. Remember, it's to help the audience appreciate your content, not so much to help you remember what comes next.

- Think of a metaphor to describe an aspect of the presentation.

- Find a complicated sentence about the topic from the internet and re-word it in simpler, more user-friendly language.

Entertaining Speech

- You have been asked to give a speech at the Royal Society of Frog Watchers. Make up a story about the subject in which you were personally involved. It doesn't have to be true!

Write out your story. Include direct speech and, if you can, include a "character" voice like an accent.

- Tell a joke about The Royal Society of Frog Watchers. (If you can do this, you are a better man, woman or child than I am. Send it in and I'll put it in the next edition.)

Impromptu Speech

Imagine that you've been asked to give a speech on one of the following topics. It needs to be about three minutes long. For each topic decide on an imagined audience. Allow yourself 15 minutes preparation time. Then make the actual speech. You can use flashcards with brief notes on them but don't use the Internet to help you research. This is what it stipulates in the LAMDA exam and you might have the same constraints in real life.

Remember that **structure is very important in an impromptu speech**. In an impromptu structure is frequently the first thing that goes out of the window; make sure it stays inside the window.

Top Tip. When you are performing the speeches that you've prepared in this very brief amount of time you will probably find that there will be occasions during the delivery when you think that you are talking rubbish. Try not to let this show. I mean try really hard. You can get away with an awful lot if people don't know that inside you are trembling.

Two men looked through prison bars the one saw mud the other saw stars

Jealousy

Should we always tell the truth

Respect

Everything happens for a reason

Is Artificial intelligence a blessing or a curse?

Sorrow

The teachers know best?

Chapter Three

Structure - Get it Organised

Research Matrerial.

Have one eye on what is important and one eye on stuff that will be particularly engaging.

Go to as many different sources as possible, look online, use books,watch documentaries.

Take a lot of care to work out what is fact and what is opinion.

You could also carry out original research of your own, interviewing people or making a survey.

Then you need to decide what to include. Don't copy anyone else's words but certainly note and be influenced by anything you read that impresses you.

Then when you have everything you think you need, organise it.

Start by summarising each piece of content in a couple of words, then make a list of the material in bullet points.

Work out what's important and what's not.

Organise

Apply your bullet points to a structure. You've really got to have a good structure. This is all about the way you order the stuff you want to say. Which, in turn, is connected to how you engage your audience.

There is a well tried and tested way of organising a speech. It's not the only way, but it's good.

Choose a topic for a speech. It could be one from the impromptu exercise, if you like. Work out what you would like to say, then think of how to summarise it in bullet points.

Apply it to the structure below.

Copy the table onto a sheet of A4. Write a couple of words to summarise each bullet point in the column on the right. You may want to leave the hook and dynamic close section blank at first. Sometimes it is much easier to think of these when you know what's happening in the rest.

Hook	
Intro and Credentials	
Overview	
3 Main Points	
Summary	
Dynamic Close	

How this structure works

Hook.

So-called because you need to hook the audience right from the very beginning; you need to get them interested. Very.

This is probably the most important part of the whole enterprise; if you are really going to nail this speech down hard, this is the hammer, mamma.

So say or do something really striking, intriguing. You probably won't think of a suitable hook until you have done your work on the body of the speech.

There does need to be a bit of what you might call **a health warning with the hook**.

And it's this: sometimes speakers are so keen to get their speech off to a dramatic or surprising start that they risk being shocking or offensive. If you are shocking or offensive you will be an overnight sensation or banned from ever speaking anywhere ever again.

Use your judgement.

<u>Introduce Yourself.</u>

Note that you do this *after* the hook. Not the other way round, as you might think. People do often begin with an introduction thinking it's polite or something but really when someone walks onto the stage and says,

Hello, my name is Felicity Fotheringhay and today I'm going to talk to you about flower arranging,

the audience really switches off quite quickly.

Even if they like flower arrangements.

And alliterative names.

Credentials.

The reason why you are a suitable person to be talking on this topic; if you're talking about cats, your credentials could be simply that you've had a lot of cats. If you're talking about a highly technical matter, your credentials will be in your qualifications and experience.

Overview.

Use sentences like:

In this talk I'm going to be explaining X, Y, and Z.

The overview is to help the audience follow the structure, to convince them that you've got yourself organised, so they know what to expect, which is reassuring both for them and for you.

The Body.

This should usually consist of **three main points.** It's difficult for people to follow a speech, much more difficult than it is to read a document where they can easily re-read anything they don't get.

With spoken delivery they've only got one chance, so you have to keep things relatively simple and three main points usually do it.

Your most important point comes first, as mentioned above, unless your three points create a narrative, when the third point will be the climax.It's helpful, too, to have discourse markers as you go along.

These are sentences that explain exactly where you are. For example:

*I've just talked about external pressures, **now I'm going to go on to look at** internal issues.*

Again it's all about helping your audience know where you are.

Summary.

Here we say something like:

So I've explained the value of x, the risks of y and the opportunities of z.

Dynamic Close.

The last bit of your speech.

Here we go for something dramatic. It's like the hook at the start.

It might be a little bit spectacular to give them something to go home with.

You have to finish strong.

You could try:

- **the bracketing technique** where you refer back to the opening, the hook, so if you use a prop at the start, you use the same prop at the end with a development or a twist.

- **Put the thing you have been talking about in a whole new massive perspective**, explaining broader applications of what you have been talking about in a way that opens up new horizons or greater significance. Maybe you have been talking about, let's say, gardening. You finish by saying something about how beautiful gardens make a positive impact everywhere, how you are contributing to a better, more beautiful world.

- **Have a Call to Action**. This is where you ask the audience to do something as a result of having listened to you. It might be to buy your book! It might be something more selfless like asking them to join a charitable effort. It should be something they can do right now.

- Or you could finish by **making a personal commitment or promise** that you are going to do something special yourself:

"I've talked a lot in my speech about the fantastic activity of mountaineering and today, I can announce that I'm setting off on a new expedition to...!

Remember, start strong and finish strong.

Exercises for Structure

Following the structure pattern described in this chapter, write out a bullet-point-list for a speech on the following topics.

If you want to take it further, write a short piece explaining why you would order your main points in the particular way that you have, how your hook would work to grab attention, what you would say in your intro and credentials to make yourself sound good so the audience feels reassured and interested to hear what you have to say.

1.   An appreciation of your favourite book, film, TV show. Remember you don't just tell the story; analyse the qualities that make it great.

2.   As if you were a school teacher, give a five minute introduction to a topic from any school subject. Make those kids interested and make it seem immediate, dynamic and interesting.

3.   Give a summing up speech as a barrister prosecuting Adil Anguish-Appleby, who has been accused of stealing money from the company he works for.

By the way, never finish a sentence with the word for. The grammar police don't like it.

Chapter Four

Create the Hook.

The following cannot be overstated:

The opening of your speech is overwhelmingly the most important part.

Make it Highly Memorable

Spend a long time on it.

Do or say something a little bit dramatic, something unexpected, something that takes them by surprise, intrigues them.

Not only does a good start interest them in the topic, it also makes them think you have given this whole speech making business some serious thought. And that flatters them and reassures them that it's not going to be boring. You've scored massive credibility points before you've really got going. They may forgive you a few dull bits along the way if you have got off to a cracking start.

And here are five useful methods:

<u>Prop.</u>

Bringing something unusual onto the stage will immediately grab your audience's attention. In an international speech competition a few years back the winning contestant came on in a full suit, shirt and tie looking very smart indeed; he then took out a pair of white underpants and put them on over his trousers. He went on to talk about bullying.

In the same competition another speaker walked very confidently to centre stage and took out a packet of cigarettes. He selected a fag and fished in his immaculate suit pocket for a lighter.

He didn't actually smoke the cigarette but it looks as if he was going to and the surprise was enough to really focus the audience's attention

A Dramatic Performance.

You could do a re-enactment of a significant part of your speech.

Example:

A member of a public speaking group in Birmingham, my home city, started his speech in the following way.

By the way, it's a coincidence that the character in the story has the same surname as me. The speaker was talking about himself but his tone of voice and the fact that he seemed to be addressing me made me jump, I can tell you.

You need to imagine the man who is making this speech going bright red in the face and yelling extremely loudly. You need to imagine this because that's what he did. And that's why I jumped out of my seat.

Venables, Laddie! Sit up straight and make yourself look respectable. You're a disgrace to the form, you're a disgrace to the school and you're an embarrassment to me, your form teacher.

Those were the words that greeted me in my first year at senior school

Ladies and gentlemen, good evening . My name is Alan Venables and today I'm going to be talking to you about bullying and how it is not always the thug on a street corner thug who is the bully. Sometimes, it's people in positions of authority.

This is how he started his speech. Thanks, Alan Venables - no relation - for that. This was such a dynamic start to his speech and had everybody focused on him and interested in what he had to say. He absolutely bellowed that first paragraph. I'm not sure how you make yourself go red in the face and I'm not sure I would recommend it, but it was very effective.

<u>Story.</u>

If you don't want to be quite as dramatic as Alan, but you still want to create an imaginative vision in the audience's mind, You could tell a good, tight, short story with clear relevance to what is to follow and which is good in its own right.

To make a story work, be sure to put in some descriptive details, particularly those that appeal to the senses.

Example

It was a really cold day and the wind was icy. I was late. Late for a job interview. An interview with ABC pharmaceuticals.

And my appearance wasn't great. Because I wanted to impress these guys, I'd put on my best suit, but I hadn't worn it for a year and since then I'd put on weight.

I was bursting out of the trousers at the waist, a button was dangling by a thread; I hadn't put on a pullover because I just thought I'd look smarter in shirt and tie, but it was so cold my nose had turned red and was dripping furiously; just before I rang the doorbell of the office block where the interview was to take place, I slipped on the ice and fell into a slushy, icy puddle, breaking the ice and getting dirty water on my already unfortunate looking shirt.

I'd been so nervous about this job interview, I built myself up into a right tizzy about it, I'd hardly slept the night before; now I was going to blow it all by looking like a complete disaster.

I looked at the plate glass door in front of me and decided to go home, forget The whole idea. It was stupid to think I could ever get a job with a company like this. Who did I think I was?

And as I turned to retrace my steps back home, I slipped on the same piece of ice, went sprawling on the pavement with the contents of my briefcase being scattered across the floor. I grazed my hand and looked at a scarlet trickle of blood oozing out. Bits of gravel mixed with the blood.

And then something happened.

I changed my mind. I thought to myself:

I'll flipping well will go in there and I'll show them. I'm blooming well good enough! The hell with it, if they don't like me they can stick it!

Those may not have been the exact words.

Five years later, I'm the chairman ABC Pharmaceuticals

Ladies and gentlemen, my name is Andrew Abluecheek, and today I want to talk to you about dealing with setbacks.

This is a good little story (even though I say so myself) for a number of reasons: it is self-contained, it's got good believable detail and has dramatic tension; it engages the listeners as they could easily imagine such difficulties happening to themselves; it links absolutely with what is to be the subject matter of the speech and, not least, it builds up what in rhetorical terms is called the ethos of the speaker.

When I say it builds up the ethos of the speaker I mean that it creates empathy for the person who is standing in front of them as well as respect. And of course it has all the other benefits of a regular hook. It gets the speech off to a great start and, as I may have mentioned before, the start is extremely important.

We will be hearing more about ethos in the section on Rhetoric.

An anecdote is often an effective way of making a point. It's what English teachers call Show Don't Tell. What they mean by this is to allow your reader, or in our case, the audience, to experience the story through actions, thoughts, senses and feelings rather than just telling them.

So for example, instead of telling the audience that a character in your story, let's call her Rishika Round-About, is greedy and rude, show her displaying these qualities,

Rishika grabbed three jam doughnuts and stuffed them into her mouth, she chewed furiously, and crumbs and jam squeezed out of the sides of her full, glistening lips and clung to her wobbling chin.

"What are you looking at, ugly chops, you never seen anyone eat their lunch before?"she yelled at the bemused onlookers.

This would be more effective than saying she ate a lot and wasn't very nice.

A story will sometimes make your point more effectively than just telling the audience what you want them to know.

Narrative Structure

There is a basic structure that almost every story follows. It goes like this:

- *Exposition or setting the scene*

- *A problem happens*

- *The characters struggle to overcome the problem*

- *Climax*

- *Denouement, the unwinding of the tension.*

When you set the scene, be as specific as possible. Name the place it happened and when it happened. Give some interesting details, preferably visual ones. You could appeal to the other senses too, sound, smell, touch taste. Especially if what you refer to triggers an emotional response.

If it's a place the audience knows, so much the better.

If you, the storyteller, were involved, this is good too.

There needs to be **something intriguing about the problem.** How will the characters or the narrator deal with this issue? Or your listeners should be wondering, why is this character behaving like this?

Make the whole thing as **vivid** as possible and as immediate.You can create a sense of immediacy by including dialogue. If you're good at doing accents or impersonations this is good detail too.

The climax is of course, the most dramatic or hilarious moment.

The denouement literally means the untying of the knot. Everything gets resolved, sorted out. It is sometimes called the resolution. It's usually here that you come to the point of the story.

Sometimes a speaker can get so carried away by their story-telling ability that they forget to make their point. This is a bad mistake and will leave the audience unsatisfied.

Make the point absolutely clear. What are they to learn from this? How should they respond?

Quotation.

If you quote someone famous or someone who is an expert, it lends you by default some of their expertise and authority.

So if you quote Shakespeare it makes you sound like you are a bit of a scholar, a bit of a poet, a bit of an intellectual; if you quote Charles Darwin it makes it seem as though science is very close to your heart. The aorta, probably.

The other thing about the quotation is that it makes it seem as if the rest of your speech is going to be based on the same kind of solid, reputable well researched expertise. A good start.

Ways to introduce your quotation.

(I hope you don't mind if I use the word quotation instead of quote. My English teacher, when I was at school, used to insist on it.

He said, "Quote is a verb, quotation is the noun."

I replied, "Could you please tell us less pedantic things, sir?"

He said, "Michael, I could tell you fewer pedantic things."

So I am going to use quotation. But don't expect me to be consistent. I am ALWAYS inconsistent.)

- The great philosopher, Bertrand Russel, is reputed to have said...

This is a good one in a couple of ways: it makes it sound as though you know quite a lot about this guy and you have a lot of respect for him. *Reputed* gets you off the hook if you have not got the quotation right.

It suggests that you are the kind of person who regularly chats to your friends about Bertrand Russell and one of them told you that this is something that BR may once have said. So you're building up quite a bit of kudos as a brainbox. Subliminally.

- When Winston Churchill said...

A good one to use for a mature, traditional audience. Makes them think you are the right sort.

- *I've always been a great admirer of (insert name of your choice. If it's someone your audience loves, so much the better) and when s/he said...*

Always been a great admirer of, makes you an expert. Then you go one step further by giving your own interpretation of the great person's idea.

- *Someone once said...*

Follow this with whatever you like. Whatever will lead nicely into your speech and is intriguing, funny or slightly shocking (I said *slightly*, take it easy, tiger.)

Startling Statistic or Statement.

Again this makes you look like an interesting and knowledgeable person, someone who holds in their head interesting information that the audience was unaware of.

They don't stop to think hey, "I bet that guy spent ages researching statistics before she found that one."

Here's one:

Did you know that the average drunk driver drives 80 times before she's caught?"

There's a bit of a twist to that one as the stereotypical idea of a drunk driver would be of a man. Changing the gender of that stereotype is maybe making a statement in its own right. This would certainly be an attention grabber.

Perhaps the point of a speech beginning in this way could be:

●   *Men pose a much greater risk than women on the roads*

- *Women pose a much greater risk than men on the roads*

- *The police need more resources*

- *Life is more risky than you think (a speech given by an insurance salesperson?)*

Here's another:

- *The Greeneland shark has an ice average lifespan of 272 years some of them can even live as long as 500 years.*

This is certainly interesting. I personally thought that the elephant was the longest living animal, or maybe a whale, or maybe Santa Claus.

I think that with a statistic like this you could easily build a speech around the idea of living your life to the full making sure that you:

don't count the years, make the years count

The sentence above, by the way, is called a chiasmus, (pronounced *kee-as-mus*). I refer you to the upcoming chapter called Rhetoric.

Rhetoric is a whole brand-new adventure just waiting to be discovered by you, a magical mystery tour of delight and delectation and I know, yes, **I've told you millions of times to stop exaggerating.**

Riddle

The riddle/puzzle-solution technique whereby the speaker starts off asking something mystifying or stating something strange, getting the audience to work out what the answer to it could be. The answer will come at the end or at some point during the course of your speech.

I like to use some of my own students' speeches as examples and here's one that used the riddle-solution formula.

The speech was made by a 10-year-old, at the time a keen follower of football. So this came right at the start of his speech. The piece was done for an exam and the examiner had no idea what the content of his piece was to be.

What does Barath have in common with Sergio Agüero?

Not much, huh? You're in for a surprise.

What does he have in common with a superstar Manchester City football player?

Barath is me and I'm 10, Sergio is 24 so it's not our age

I'm from Birmingham the United Kingdom,

Sergio is from Argentina.

And Sergio is an amazingly talented football player

Barath is not. well not yet anyway.

So what do we have in common?

Well it's this...

Barath had been standing with his hands behind his back; at this point he brought them round to the front and he was holding a very stylish looking football boot.

It turns out that the famous footballer has given his name to a particular brand and type of boot and this is the one that Barath used to play football at the weekend.

His speech went on to describe in detail the gifts and talents of his favourite footballer with close reference to the boot. (Apparently kids' football boots are now designed according to the position they play. Who knew?)

You can easily see that this intriguing opening was way more effective than if he had said, "Good morning, my name is Barath and today I'm going to talk to you about Sergio Aguero."

Snoreville, right?

Some Further Examples of Hooks from my own Students' Speeches

This from a tennis coach, who walked onto the stage with a racket and ball. He looked as if he was going to actually do a tennis serve, but let the ball drop to the floor at the last moment.

Did you really think I would hit that ball in your direction? Of course not. But if I had, it would have come at you (pointing to someone in the audience) at 120 m.p.h.

"Good morning, ladies and gentlemen, my name is _____ . I've been a professional tennis coach for 10 years and today, I'm going to talk to you about the amazing joy that is the ace and how you can achieve it

- An environmental company executive wanted to impress upon an audience - whom she knew to be sceptical about global warming - the magnitude of the problem. She arranged for a table to be on stage. And for it to be covered in rubbish: empty crisp packets, drink cans etc. She walked on stage, apologised for the mess, then swept it all on to the floor and covered it with a blanket. She said,

There, we can't see it now, so it's gone away, hasn't it. It doesn't matter. I mean, I don't know about you but I just hate seeing litter just left lying about but, secretly, as soon as it's all brushed away, swept under the carpet was *hidden under the sofa well, frankly, I just don't care anymore.*

She paused for a moment then said.

I'm sorry if that was a gimmicky way to start. But that's what we as a nation are doing every day. Every day, but on a massive scale.

My name is _____ etc.

I advised this client to perform this as if it was real, she really did want the rubbish out of the way and what she was saying wasn't part of her speech at all. This created a sort of tension amongst the audience; they were thinking "oh my gosh, that's not a very professional way to start a speech or is she just doing the best thing in the circumstances?"

So there was a feeling of slight embarrassment and awkwardness in the house. Then when the speaker revealed that it actually was a deliberate part of her presentation, a metaphor for what she was going to go on to say, there was a collective sigh of relief and a smile on the face of most audience members, an appreciative smile - they were actually thinking "**This woman is a good public speaker that was a clever way to begin, this speech is going to be good.**"

- A speech coach, not unlike me, was at a breakfast meeting for network opportunities and as a newcomer to the group was asked to give a three minute presentation. He, or me, actually, began in hushed tones,

There is a group of people not far from here, in fact within a five mile radius, who are living in fear. I mean they are terrified. They couldn't sleep last night, many of them. It seems hard that in a civilised country like this, that this group of people should be put through what they are experiencing. Yet it happens all the time. For these are people who, this morning, possibly even right now, are going to have to stand up and...give a presentation.

I have in fact given the above introduction a few times, maybe five or six times, at courses I have run. It works really well. I'm a bit worried though that I may one day give it to an audience who have already heard it. Always gets a laugh and I love it when the audience looks fascinated and slightly troubled at the start.

It's a similar tactic to the Rubbish On The Table stunt. Creates a sense of confusion, then it's revealed it to be an apt and perhaps amusing way to open.

So be bold, be adventurous, start with that bang.

For goodness sake don't walk on the stage and say

hello my name is Anita Angelpoise and today I'm going to talk to you about fly fishing

Even if they like fly fishing you probably lost them at "and today I'm going to talk to you about…"

But just like the fly fisherwoman, you need to be careful with your hook.

You want it to be dramatic but don't be shocking or offensive. Take care.

Exercises for The Hook

For each of the following scenarios make up several dramatic openings. Make sure you have thought through how it would link to your speech. Look at the different types of hook mentioned in this chapter and use as many as you can.

You are giving a speech to senior citizens about the benefits of gym membership

You are headteacher at a school open day addressing prospective students and their parents.

You are about to present the summing up in a case for the defence of a serial criminal.

Chapter Five

Script

Why Script?

I know some people don't like to write a script because they much prefer their presentation to be spontaneous. They think that they are really good at speaking off the cuff, just with a bit of a plan and sometimes it's true that they are extremely good.

Some people just have a kind of natural skill to do that. Also, many Speech and Drama teachers actually tell their students not to work from a script because they are committed to the idea of spontaneity arising from non scripted work - bullet points only.

And certainly there is a risk that if the material has not been thoroughly internalised it will **sound** like a script.

But if they really wanted to be 100% totally, absolutely, utterly and completely sure that they were going to give a good presentation, then I would recommend that a speaker writes a script.

The way most likely to ensure a great performance is to have a script written, to memorise it thoroughly and to perform it with conviction.

You've already partly embedded a sense of spontaneity by speaking your ideas before you wrote it.

Here's a thing.

There is a neat old saying:

it's not what you say, it's the way that you say it

Like many old sayings, it's not true.

Well, not really.

The truth is - and this is not as neat -

it's a huge amount about what you say but the way that you say it is also very important, sometimes more important, depending on the circumstances which will obviously vary contextually

No, that's not a pretty sentence but it's true.

In this book we are looking at what you say and the way that you say it, with both being of roughly equal importance in speech making.

Usually!

Now, here's another thing.

Creating a script for a speech is not like writing an essay; it's a lot more messy, the preparation is a lot less structured. Mainly this is because when you give a speech, you want it to sound natural, not like an essay. If you write it in the same way you would an assignment, you may find that it sounds pretentious when spoken in front of an audience, it sounds too formal.

People won't like you. They may think you're a fake or just stuffy.

And here's yet another thing. The last one for a bit.

You need to decide this pretty early on in the process: **how do I want my audience to respond to this?**

Nail this down first.

Then keep referring yourself back to this as you get your script together.

And how do I get my script together? I hear you ask.

So you need to do several things at more or less the same time:

research ideas, then scribble those ideas down, then say them out loud, then write them down sort of neatly. Then *say them out loud again while walking around pretending you are in front of an audience. Then start to put your notes in some sort of order, then cross out rubbish ideas and add new good ones*

Set the above to Repeat.

Now, I said "sort of" neatly because it's a mistake to write your speech too neatly too soon; it will look like the finished article and you may be tempted to stick with it just because it is so neat. But your speech needs to feel spontaneous; when it's spoken, it needs to have the ring of true, natural speech.

So what I think you should do is get a whole bunch of ideas together and then keep alternating between saying them out loud and scribbling down notes.

Your written notes feed into your walking-around-performing;

your walking-around-performing feeds into your written notes.

Over time, you make your performance and your writing incrementally better, more polished, until ultimately you have your speech.

So rehearse your speech using bullet points and improvise. Have a piece of paper and pen next to you and stop occasionally to make notes of things that sound wrong or things that you need to remember to change later. But don't spend more than a few seconds note taking.

The first two or three times that you rehearse, don't worry too much about putting on a performance, make it fairly low-key, don't put too much effort into it. You're just getting used to finding your way around the material; you don't want to be put off by trying to impress the imagined audience.

Then, as you go on, to your third or fourth run through, make it more and more like a performance.

Try to visualise the room in which you will be performing, act as if there really is an audience and concentrate on communicating to them. The more vividly you imagine their presence, the more effective your speech will become.

As well as visualising the audience, picture yourself being very good in your delivery and the audience responding positively. This lifts your performance and actually goes a long way to allaying your nerves. I always like to rehearse alone at first, as I feel free to be very expressive in my delivery. If I go over the top I can always calm it down later.

But sooner or later, preferably later, you will want to write a script. In my opinion. Because when you have a script you can be absolutely sure that the words you deliver will be the best they could be. There will be no chance of you saying something silly or inappropriate. There is no chance that you miss out important details.

Your script will now arise fairly naturally out of the rehearsals that you have been doing; you won't need to think about it too hard.

But…

Be ready to respond to events as they happen. Yes, you've got your script, and, yes, I know I have banged on and on about how useful it is but only a silly person sticks with the words regardless of what goes on around them.

If something unexpected happens during the course of your presentations, react to it, say something about it.

In assembly at the school I worked at in the eighties, I was talking to the students about alcohol. The message I was conveying could be boiled down to:

most adults in our society do drink, but you have to be careful to keep it under control. And if you can't then life can go badly wrong

Along those lines. And I was laying it on pretty thick.

Five minutes into the assembly, the siren of an ambulance could be heard as it screeched past the school and I said,

For all we know, that ambulance could right now be on its way to someone suffering from an accident that happened from drinking too much.

The effect was electric, though I say so myself.It brought home the reality of the situation:

this is a potential problem for us right here, right now

So it made my message stronger.

I could do this because I was so confident that I knew what I was going to say in the rest of my presentation. It was all absolutely mapped out in my mind, so deviating from the track was no problem. I could easily come back to it again.

So adapting to the actual situation is important.

To an extent you can, and should, prepare your script for the particular audience and the unique time of its delivery.

Use the Active Voice

The **passive** voice is where you say something like: *the machine has been broken*, the **active** voice is when you say *Paul broke the machine*.

So it is clear who is responsible for the action of the verb.

Sometimes if you use the passive voice it looks as if you are hiding something. And as such it can be like putting a little barrier between you and the audience.

Make Speech fit Audience

So we don't just throw the words randomly down on the paper, we focus our thoughts very much on the nature of the live event ahead of us.

Make a point of the **unique nature** of the event. Emphasising that this is a one off occasion. An audience doesn't really like to feel that you are just trotting out a speech that you've delivered dozens of times before in exactly the same way to dozens of other audiences. Even if they know this is true, they would appreciate it if you make some reference to local events or local places, explaining the particular relevance to them.

Consider who your audience is

- *Do they have shared interest or experience or knowledge?*

If so, you adjust your language accordingly. If they are all very knowledgeable in some scientific field for example then it's okay to use language particular to that area. If not then you need to avoid jargon.

- *Do they have shared values or beliefs?*

In this case, assuming you want to win them over, you can make it clear in your script that you share these views; you can use the kind of words and phrases that mark them out as a special group thereby making you seem as if you belong.

- *Are they all at the same kind of educational level, same age, or all live in the same area?*

Make plenty of references that will have a resonance for this group. If you are a part of this group yourself, you can make a point of this commonality. If not, then you should mention the lack of commonality but finding a way to make it a good thing - you could say it helps you be objective maybe.

Other ways of emphasising the singularity of this occasion might be to refer to the weather, the time of day or if you can find a way of pointing out that this is an anniversary of some kind,

It's exactly 6 years to this very day that I stood on a stage very similar to this one and... my word how things

have changed. Little then did I think that I would be here in these circumstances

Or,

Today is very special because...

It's all part of the game of keeping the audience engaged. Remember that at all times you are striving to prevent them from thinking that this is just going to be some humdrum, run of the mill regular boring thing.

This is just one more trick in your tool box. It's always good to have tricks in your tool box and mixed metaphors in your pantry.

Talk Their Language

Whenever you have an audience in front of you they are almost certainly a group that has something in common that distinguishes them from other groups of people.

If you want to get them on your side and if you want to do something that's really good for your Ethos (see Rhetoric) you need to adjust your choice of words to appeal to their idiosyncratic quality as a group.

So it might be that they all live in the same area. So you could say things like

here in Derbyshire, I know that this issue is of great relevance to you...

Maybe they are all shift workers who work at night on frequent occasions so you could say:

when you are going out to work just at the time when everyone else is thinking of going to bed, you will be aware...

If you have an audience of medics you could throw this line in:

a close personal friend of mine is a doctor, and she was saying to me only yesterday...

They will like you if you do this. If you are a Speech and Drama student and you are at a grade where you have to do an impromptu speech, I find that this is a particularly helpful technique.

Let's call it the referring to the **audience's idiosyncratic experience technique**.

It makes the examiner think that you are really taking the whole idea seriously, creating the impression that you are really visualising an audience in front of you. Obviously the technique works in a real world situation too.

Let's take it a step further. When you know you're going to be making a speech to a particular group of people, do some research and find out things that are relevant to them only as a group. Look at the internet. They have a website, do they have a brochure? Are there articles about them in the newspaper or in magazines? Take a close look at their literature. Are **there phrases or words that keep cropping up their materials** that you don't find elsewhere so much?

If so, these are the buzzwords of this group.

Unashamedly steal these words and use them in your speech. Now you really are talking their language and this makes them much more likely to engage with you.

Swearing in a Speech.

Don't.

Unless you are a stand up comedian or an extremist politician talking to a group of hard core supporters and you want to whip them up into a frenzy.

Stand ups usually get away with it because it's kind of expected of them and because the audience likes to think that they are "off duty," they're letting their hair down and they appreciate the irreverence.

But even with stand ups it can be counter productive if people think it's an excuse for not having much really good material.

Extremist politicians get away with it (sometimes) because it shows the extreme emotions they are trying to engender in their audience.

So if you're not one of them in one of these two categories forget it, don't do it, you just don't know who in your audience will be offended and your objective is to engage not to alienate. Don't risk it.

Exercises for Script

- Rewrite the following paragraph making it much more audience friendly, that is to say less formal and more direct.

After a lengthy consultation process with stakeholders and all parties with a vested interest it has been decided that henceforth we will be adopting more lenient measures. Those members of the audience present today who disagree with this decision will be invited to make their feelings known at a later stage.

- Research a company or organisation that interests you. Try to find out what their **buzzwords** are. That is to say words or phrases they use often, more often than is usual. Make up three or four sentences from a speech that you might give to them, incorporating these words as naturally as you can.

- Imagine that you have to give a talk on coastal erosion. Or some such.

Something a bit technical. You have to give the speech twice, once to a group of eleven year olds and then later to a group of A level students. Write about the same aspect, the same material but use audience appropriate language.

Chapter Six

Rhetoric

Most people have heard of the word rhetoric in one of two contexts: the rhetorical question; or when someone is being accused of using "empty rhetoric."

At school you will almost certainly have been taught what a rhetorical question is.

Well, you have, haven't you?

It's actually a pity that this is the only part of rhetoric that you have been taught about; maybe schools have missed a trick here. For a couple of thousand years rhetoric was taught in schools, I mean it was actually on the school syllabus for every school in England.

Why did they think it was so important?

Ok, ok I'll stop the rhetorical questions.

Or will I?

Yes, why did they think it was so important that the children of the rich and the children of the middle classes were taught rhetoric as if it were just every bit as important as mathematics, science and witchcraft?

Well, okay, yes, they did later discover that witchcraft was a load of tosh but rhetoric most certainly wasn't.

Actually rhetoric means the **art of persuasive speaking**. And every single technique used, and believe me there are a lot, is still absolutely useful today. It is, as you might have guessed, most suitable for a persuasive speech. But it has its part to play in any kind of speech.

So if you don't know anything about it you're a bit of a disadvantage when making a speech.

A little bit of history. Okay, if you don't like history, move on.

But if you do, here goes. In Ancient Greece, roughly two and a half thousand years ago, they had a democracy. This was pretty much the first time there had been a democracy, a type of organisation where people choose their own rules and choose the people who make the rules. You knew that? Sorry.

So if you were the kind of person who actually quite fancied the idea of being the person who made up the rules then you would have to persuade people to vote for you. Note the word **persuade** there.

So all budding politicians had to give speeches in which they tried to persuade people to vote for them. It became a highly competitive business as apparently lots of people wanted to be politicians. Don't ask me why, but they did.

In this competitive environment, it soon became clear that persuading people wasn't just a case of having the best argument. It was also down to how you organised your case or arranged your words to win people over. Not everyone who wanted to be a politician was very good with words and so guess what? They hired people who were good with words to help them out.

The first group of people who helped them out with words called themselves **Sophists**. I don't know why. Google it. And email me when you find out, thanks for saving me the trouble.

Sophists used to listen to the person who wanted to make a speech and then they would write that speech for them and tell them how to say it. They would charge quite a bit of money for this service.

They had spotted a gap in the market. Very enterprising.

After a while they got a bit of a bad reputation. It was said that they were more interested in making money than in the truth; perish the thought of anyone doing anything like that these days. I'm naming no names.

But because it was said they were more interested in making money than in the truth, the word Sophistry gained a bit of a stigma.

And being described as sophisticated, whilst it might be a compliment these days, was a definite insult back then.

A bit later on, maybe 500 years later, a guy called Aristotle decided to put things right.

He thought it was important that people were able to persuade others eloquently and he worked out the best ways of doing it.

He wrote it all down in a book called *The Art of Rhetoric*. Man, that is a hard book to read, and to save you the trouble, I'm summarising some of the best bits here.

There are many techniques employed in rhetoric.

Here, I'm going to talk about two main areas:

- three overarching principles

- and several neat little ways of using language.

The Three Pillars of Rhetoric.

Logos

Logos means convincing people of a point by appealing to their brains, as opposed to their hearts, giving them logical arguments.

Logos will often include statistics, numbers, facts. You don't just state the facts, you show how they support the point that you are trying to make.

Let's say that you were a great believer in HS2 to the high-speed train that at the time of writing it is planned to build taking passengers from London to the north of England at, yes, high speed. It's very expensive to build this, it's costing billions of pounds and some people don't like the idea to say the least, in fact they hate the idea. This is for a number of reasons and they include environmental destruction and of course the high cost which they say could be better spent on other things like for example the NHS.

But to come back to you and the case that you, in this hypothetical situation, are arguing for. You are saying that this train line should be built. So when it comes to using logos you would perhaps refer to the economic benefits that would follow on from the HS2, you would have a folder with you which you might wave around a little bit, and inside you would say,

The data is from research undertaken by a highly reputable statistical analysis company, and they have worked out the exact profits and benefits that would come to local communities from the railway line.

Three Pillows of Rhetoric by Lasa

Ethos

Ethos, in the rhetorical sense of the word, means persuading people by the strength of your personality. Your audience is much more likely to be open to persuasion if they like you, if they think **they can trust you**.

If they think you **share their values,** think you're the sort of person who knows what the **right thing is to do** on a variety of different occasions, they are more likely to be persuaded.

They also want to believe that you have **their interests at heart**. So some of your speech should be about making them think you're a good person or that you are **the sort of person they could happily work with**.

Let's stick with the example used above. How are you going to deploy ethos?

Let's make the task that you're facing a little bit harder. Let's say that your audience consists of people who live along the route of the proposed train line and some of them will have to have their houses demolished if the project goes ahead.

So this is a tough audience indeed and it may be impossible to win all of them over. Or any of them. But if you approach carefully, you may least be able to have some impact on the hostility.

You might begin by convincing them that you have many of the same values that they have. Perhaps you might slip in a comment about how you dropped your children off at school before you came to the meeting. Maybe you will refer to the community in which you live yourself and stress how important you think it is to live in a close-knit community.

And from there, working very carefully and selecting your words with sensitivity, you might move on to explicitly say that because of your own background, you are fully aware of the difficulties that people are facing and assure them that your values are the same as theirs; you will be doing everything with the construction company to be responsive to their needs and wishes to retain their community togetherness.

Another example of building ethos, came in a speech I'm currently working on with my student, Arjun. He wants to do a piece about contemporary music, those styles of music like "Drill" and Rap. There is often bad language and violent imagery in this music. He is imagining a hostile audience as he tries to explain his views, which are:

• He sees **nothing wrong** with anti establishment political comments in music

• He sees **nothing wrong** with swearing in music provided young children don't hear it

- He **does disapprove** of lyrics which encourage violence.

He has decided to put the third point first, because he thinks the audience will agree with this one. So he is building his ethos here, by making the audience see that he shares (at least some of) their values, before going on to the points they may find harder to take. So this is his strongest point from the view of the audience.

Pathos

With pathos you arouse their **emotions, feelings.** People often make decisions based on what their emotions tell them, then they justify it rationally later.

Let's stay with the not inconsiderable problem of persuading people that it's okay to have their homes demolished.

Tricky.

What we might do is use the **sunlit uplands** technique. This is where you paint an idealised image of a future time of happiness, prosperity and good fortune.

There will come a time, and it's close, where this community will be more beautiful even than it is already, the resources pouring into the area will bring unimaginable benefits to all. A new community centre with facilities unrivalled anywhere in the region: a library, a beautiful pub, local businesses enjoying a prosperity that until now could only be dreamed of.

Winston Churchill used the phrase during the Second World War when he contrasted what the future would be like if Hitler was defeated with what it would be like if he won.

Boris Johnson also borrowed the idea during the British referendum campaign:

we find that a door has magically opened in our lives... we can see the sunlit Meadows beyond. I believe we would be mad not to take this once-in-a-lifetime chance to walk through that door

Working an audience's feelings is something that many speakers do, particularly when there is a very large audience.

Another way of doing this is by telling a story and making the audience **feel the sensations** of being in the story. So, if, for example, you wanted your colleagues or employees to feel anger, rather than just telling them the reasons why they should be angry, give them a vivid story which illustrates your point.

The more they feel they are personally involved in the story or that you personally witnessed it the more powerful the impact.

One thing to note is that rhetoric is much less effective if people notice that you are using it.

This is when may sense they are being played with and then you'll lose it. I wouldn't fancy your chances of getting out of that church hall.

Rhetorical Devices

A rhetorical device is a way of arranging words, phrases or sentences in such a way as to be particularly persuasive.

They frequently have a sort of aesthetic attractiveness, a pleasant sound, and it is this very quality that makes them seem to contain truth.

Another appealing aspect of rhetorical devices is that they are often very memorable, meaning that the speaker's words stay in the audience's mind.

And so his words may be quoted, giving the speaker further reach for his words, extending his influence.

There are hundreds of rhetorical devices; here are a few useful ones.

The Chiasmus

This is where the second half of the sentence is a mirror image of the first half.

For example:

We make our habits and then our habits make us.

Work to live, don't live to work.

Don't ask what your country can do for you; ask what you can do for your country.

Yes, Kennedy. Politicians love a bit of rhetoric and often consciously apply it.

Anaphora

This is a device that is very effective if used sparingly; this is a device that can have a cumulatively persuasive effect; this is a device that can make you sound Churchillian.

It's where you repeat the opening phrase in successive sentences or phrases as above.

Winston Churchill used the phrase "we shall fight" eight times in a famous speech at the start of the Second World War.

My mother heard it on the radio in 1940, just as a side note for you.

People say that the effect of that speech on the English was amazing and my mum agrees. "Everyone was a bit shocked, but in a good way, we thought 'Oh, we're not going to give up then, we are going to roll our sleeves up and win." Rhetoric for you.

Hyperbole - exaggeration for effect - is another device, sometimes paired with alliteration. As in:

I'd rather be dead in a ditch than delay Brexit.

At least I'm presuming this was hyperbole as the speaker was not subsequently found dead in a ditch.

Symploce

Here we have entered the territory of high rhetoric. It's defined like this: successive clauses of the same first and last words.

An example will make this clear. This is from Barack Obama:

In the struggle for peace and justice we cannot walk alone. In the struggle for opportunity and equality we cannot walk alone. In the struggle to heal this nation and repair this world we cannot walk alone.

Rhetorical Contrast

This is often a highly effective way of emphasising your point.

Here is a famous examples from Neil Armstrong:

That's one small step for man; and one giant leap for mankind.

You don't have to be an astronaut to use rhetorical contrast.

You can say things like:

We are only being asked to make a small change but we are going to create a massive response.

That's how they do things in that company over there but this is how we do things

Rhetorical questions

Asking a rhetorical question is a way of getting the audience to reflect on the answer and thereby get them to engage with your speech.

There are actually quite a lot of different types. Here are just a few.

First there is the rhetorical question where the answer is glaringly obvious. It confirms the point that you want to make and thereby emphasises it.

can we really allow this distressing state of affairs to continue?"

Then there is the rhetorical question which is just to promote reflection and contemplation and the answer is not necessarily obvious. Maybe there is no answer:

What is the meaning of life?"

Sometimes the speaker feigns innocence of the answer but in such a way that the audience sees he is being ironic.

Like when, in the play, Julius Caesar, Mark Anthony tells the crowd that he once offered Caesar a "kingly crown" and says Caesar refused it three times.

Did this in Caesar seem ambitious?

So the answer is obviously no, anyone who is ambitious will want a kingly crown. I know I would. In this way Mark Anthony demonstrates that it was wrong to kill Julius Caesar on the basis that he was ambitious. So he wins them over. The rhetorical question is a persuasive device.

Yet another type of rhetorical question is where the speaker goes a bit theatrical and asks a question and then answers it himself. It becomes a mini quasi dialogue.

Are we just going to roll over and give up?

Speaker pauses dramatically.

No, we're going to roll up our sleeves and get on.

There is more word play in that sentence above, by the way. What is it called?

Send me an email to tell me.

mike@or8.co.uk

<u>Final Thought on Rhetoric</u>

Do you remember I said you have to be a little bit careful with the hook?

Well you have to be a little bit careful with the rhetoric as well.

It was our man, Aristotle, who said that when it becomes obvious to your audience that you are deliberately using rhetoric, it loses its power and undermines you.

So try to be subtle.

Usually it's the case that the bigger the crowd, the more effective rhetoric is, as you engender a corporate response. Think football crowds.

So it's probably not a good idea to go all rhetorical when you are presenting to a group of three.

Three thousand, yes, but three, no, no, they will think you've just gone way over the top.

Exercises on Rhetoric

Imagine that you are trying to persuade members of a local county council that a certain pot of money should be spent on a theatre rather than a gym. Or the other way round if you are one of these fitness freak people as opposed to an arty-farty type.

Think of three different ways you could try to persuade them.

- one of them should be demonstrating ethos

- one of them showing logos

- and the third one using pathos.

So that means of course one using your personality, one using up your logic and one playing on their emotions.

Rhetorical Devices

Chiasmus.

Remember this is the one where the second half of the sentence is a mirror image (almost) of the first half.

Complete these:

- *Bad men live that they may eat and drink, whereas...*

- *We make our habits and then...*

Now make up a few of your own. Topics could include any number of abstract nouns: beauty, hope, success etc.

Chapter Seven
Vocal Variety

In the field of history, one of the sentences most frequently quoted is:

An eye for an eye ends up making the world blind

Mahatma Gandhi

In the field of literature, one of the phrases most frequently quoted is:

to be or not to be that is the question

William Shakespeare

In the field of public speaking, and if there were such a field it be a very lovely one full of pretty flowers, one of the phrases most frequently quoted is:

In any communication, 55% of the meaning conveyed comes through facial expression, 38% comes from the tone of voice and only 7% comes from the words actually spoken

A.Daft-Speaking-Coach

There are three interesting things about the last one: one, it's a misquote, second it's hardly ever true; third plenty of speech coaches say it is true.

So where does it come from? It comes from a very small scale experiment carried out by Albert Mehrabian, a professor of psychiatry, in 1967. It was a very small scale experiment indeed. On the basis of this experiment he came out with the statistics above. The weird thing is that people extrapolate from this the idea that it is true of all oral communication at all times.

Hmm.

Let's take an example. Say to the next person you see, "My gosh, you're ugly, I'd hate to look like that." But say it with a big smile on your face and in a really, really friendly happy tone of voice; use gestures that are open and warm.

Now if the person you are speaking to responds to you in a friendly, cheerful manner, you will know that the majority of the meaning of your words were indeed conveyed through facial expression, tone of voice and gesture and that the actual words spoken didn't really matter.

If on the other hand they slap your face and say that you are far uglier than they are, you will know that your words, the actual words spoken, counted for a lot more than 7% of the meaning.

I mention this because I've got a bee in my bonnet about it, having been on many courses about presentation skills and I know that lots of instructors say this.

Maybe it's a bit ironic after that, but now I'm now going to go on to tell you just how very important your tone of voice and body language are: massively important but it depends on the circumstances.

The way your speech is received depends an awful lot on how you say things; it is possible for someone to have a speech which on paper looks really boring and because of the way they deliver it they make it sound great.

Mind you, you need to be good to do this.

But then again, we are trying to make you good, not just any old good, but really really good.

You can make a fairly dull speech exciting if you work creatively with movement and tone of voice and probably tweak the script a little bit.

So let's get on and talk about how to make your voice interesting.

If you're really serious about *Nailing Public Speaking*, then you need to explore the potential in your voice for expressiveness.

Your tone of voice can convey so much meaning and dramatically affect the way that people respond to your message.

Most of the time it's purely instinctive of course. You're feeling sad so you take on a sad tone of voice, you're feeling happy so you take on a happy tone, you're feeling absolutely furious so you, well, you get the idea. It just comes naturally, it's not something you think about.

But any staged performance is just that - staged. It's a heightened version of you, it's a version of you that you want to linger in people's memories. Not generally the case in a normal conversation.

And if you just allow your tone of voice to be completely spontaneous, it may be that you won't get the best effect from your voice. It may be that this won't be the best way of conveying the message.

You have got time to prepare your presentation , so you can prepare all aspects of it including what is the best way to say each individual sentence.

Basically there are four ways in which you can change your tone of voice: you can vary the **pitch**, the **pace**, the **power** - we could call this volume but we would lose the alliteration which would be a shame - and you can include dramatic **pauses**.

Shreya and Bruno

Now regarding the use of the voice, I'm going to go for another sporting analogy here. Let's suppose you're a triathlon athlete. So you have to run for a bit, well actually quite a lot, then you have to swim for a bit, yes, quite a lot and then you have to cycle, erm, quite a lot.

You learned to run when you were about three years old, learned to swim when you were let's say, eight years old and learned to ride a bike around about the same time. So the junior version of you would, thereafter, just do all of those things without even thinking about them. And it would be fine; you'd run, you would swim, you would ride a bike.

But you sure would be no triathlete. You would only become that when you had learned technique and of course practised a lot.

Where am I going with all of this? You may ask. And I'll tell you.

I'm going in the direction of vocal variety in your speech.

Yes, we know that you can speak words and we know that people can hear them and we know that you change the pitch, pace, pause and power elements of your voice from time to time to make yourself a little bit more expressive.

But when you become a public speaker you are on the road to becoming the language equivalent of the triathlete and it's good to have a little bit of technique.

Fortunately for you it is significantly easier than becoming an Olympic champion.

The first thing to do is to take your speech and have a look at practising saying some sentences in a variety of different ways, changing any one of The Four Ps.

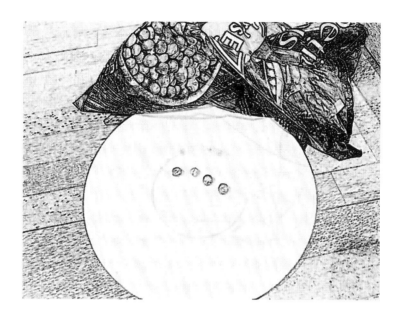

The Four Peas

You often find it quite surprising the different effects you can get by making changes.

So to go back to the comparison of the athlete, what you're doing here, when you examine your script in detail, looking at vocal changes that you can make, is the equivalent of the athlete who is looking over the particular terrain that she has to cover, looking at tricky little bends in the road, etc. Is there a pothole in the road? You're finding ways to get the job done in the best way possible.

Should you pause here or there? Say this bit more loudly or speed up the pace?

But of course the athlete doesn't just race at one time in one place. They will have needed to have built up technique.

I actually think we've probably got a little bit too far with this metaphor so let's just come back to speech and drama. It's a good idea to build up vocal technique and to understand the different ways in which the four Ps work.

Pitch.

The main reasons for changing the pitch when you're speaking are: to emphasise words, to show a change of thought or to show an emotional involvement.

Let's think first about emphasis. When you want words or phrases to stand out in your speech you can do so by using a change of pitch amongst other things. So you can change to a higher or lower note on the word you want emphasised. Here is an example

Take this sentence

I'm going to the park with Jane tonight.

You will see that changing the pitch on the different syllables here will emphasise a word and thereby change the meaning.

I'm... boasting that your friend is not going to the park with Jane tonight

Go... no one is going to stop me

Park... excitedly, I'm not going to the circus

Now think about how pitch indicates mood or a change of thought. A higher pitch usually suggests excitement, a lower pitch, seriousness.

Take this sentence:

It was so exciting to arrive in this great, glittering metropolis. But later that day I saw a much darker side of the city.

Say it out loud and use a high pitch for the first sentence and change the pitch rather dramatically to a lower pitch for the second sentence.

Don't worry if it sounds a little bit over the top right now; we are just making the point.

Newsreaders very frequently have quite pronounced changes of tone when they go from bad news to more cheerful news, which they sometimes do at the end of a bulletin just to lift the mood with a little bit of a good news story to send you to bed without nightmares.

Pace.

A change of pace can also be used to emphasise words and to suggest emotional changes.

So first, how does the pace affect emphasis?

Normally the way to emphasise the word using pace is to stretch it to take longer over the delivery of a particular syllable. To slow down the pace.

Here is an example:

My chances of jumping over this gate are unlikely

Say it out loud, emphasising certain syllables by slowing them down; by stretching them you will see how changing the emphasis changes the meaning implied.

Chances...I'm probably going to need medical treatment if I even try

Jump...I should probably just open it and walk through rather than showing off

This... I could jump over that gate (possibly Jane's gate) easily

Gate...I'll jump over the little wall instead and keep some dignity

Unlikely...definitely not easy, but what the heck

The thing here, in all this gate to-jump-or-not-to-jumping, is that you can make a word stand out by saying it more slowly.

Now we will take a look at changing the pace to reflect changes of emotion.

Generally, a faster pace reflects passion, a slower pace indicates considered thought or maybe sadness, dejection.

Try saying each of these sentences quickly, then slowly.

Yes, I've won the lottery!

I've still got three hours of homework left.

See?

Pause

You can pause dramatically before you say an important word or phrase, or you can pause after that same word or phrase. Or both.

The idea with the pause **before** the important word is that you make the audience intrigued to create a little bit of suspense.

*And today I can announce that the winner of the competition is (**pause**)Florrie Forgoodnessake*

And then if you want to make the audience reflect upon what you have just said then you pause **after** the key word.

Here's an example taken from a speech of one of my students, Niya. It's on the topic of vegetarianism.

*In your lifetime you will eat 7000 animals. 7000. (**pause**.) That is a desperately shocking statistic.*

Power.

Loud volume usually means greater emotion and force, but the same effect can sometimes be gained by being dramatically, but audibly, quiet.

As with pitch and pace, speaking the words more loudly or rather picking out individual words to speak more loudly than others, is a way of emphasising them. If you use power in isolation to emphasise those words it does end up sounding rather aggressive and lacking sensitivity.

A great technique that you can try is the **vocal climax**. This is where you have a series of sentences or phrases with the last one being the most powerful. So you use the four Ps in combination starting slowly, pausing and speaking quietly and you progressively ramp up the expression by losing the pauses, heightening the pitch and raising the power.

Be careful you don't sound too hysterical by the end of this, by the way.

Try it on the following three sentences

What the opposition party did was unacceptable. They set up fake social media accounts to undermine this. They blatantly and unashamedly lied. **(make sure you really belt out the *lied*)**

To conclude this section on voice and vocal variety, I think you need a two pronged attack. But using the same weapons.

One is to focus on the particular script that you've got, the other is to look at and develop expression generally.

For the particular script, select important lines from the text and experiment with vocal variety. You never want to sound over the top, or theatrical, so don't push it too far, but do think of yourself as a bit of an actor and explore the range of your voice in the context of this script.

So, for example, you might think to yourself, "I will try a dramatic pause here," or "I'll speak a little bit more slowly."

Just try it and see; sometimes it's really astonishing the effects that you can get.

Then for developing expression generally, like the athlete who needs to train in a variety of circumstances, like, for example, not just on the track but in the gym, you should think about reading different materials out loud from time to time and just push your voice, try things out see what you can do, see how your voice can make the material come to life.

Try reading stories to children (real ones if you can find a couple) and do the voices. Give Gruffalo a real character-voice, give the wicked witch a wicked voice and give Snow White a real cute little voice.

You're getting double bonus points here, you're doing your sistererly/brotherly/parental duties (if they're your sibs or kids) and you are developing your vocal expression.

To finish this chapter, here are a few practical tips about vocal variety

- Don't let your voice fade away and drop down at the end of sentences. People do this all of the time in normal conversation and it doesn't matter. But in the stage performance it really is very much better to make an effort to avoid it. So try doing the opposite. When you come to the last couple of words of a sentence, project them a little bit more forcefully than seems quite natural and maybe raise the pitch.

- Most of the time in a speech it is better to speak more slowly than you generally would. People expect this. And it unquestionably aids and facilitates understanding.

- Sometimes you can indicate that your speech has come to an end by your **intonation**. You don't need to say something lame like, "Thank you for listening."

Make the pitch of your voice high on your last few words and speak at a very slow tempo; then bring your voice to a low pitch to make the end really dramatic.

When you go to a high pitch it sort of feels incomplete and then the sudden contrast in pitch emphasises that it's a close.

I feel that was slightly inarticulate so I'm going to ask a friend. Anyway, the words could go like this:

(Moving to a high pitch and going slowly) *and that is* (go still higher and slower) *how you* (still higher and slower) *chew* (pause, bring the pitch crashing down now and say this last word quicly but clealry *gum!*

I asked my friend, Gary Spruce, who is a musical kind of person, how this might be described in musical terms. He said, "Hmm, I *think* you might be talking about Crescendo-Ralentando-Lungo-Pause-Accentuto."

If you think you've got a better way of explaining the above, let me know. mike@or8.co.uk

I'll put it in the updated version and give you a pat on the back and send you a box of chocolates. Or flowers. Your choice.

Exercise to Explore Voice

Whilst this book is all about how to deliver speeches and presentations, it's useful sometimes to look at **dramatic** texts. They give us a vehicle to explore what we can do technically without being worried about whether the content is right for a speech.

I've included here a monologue from Tennessee Williams' play *The Glass Menagerie.* It's a male character, though it really doesn't matter about gender as it's an exercise to start thinking about developing your range linked to emotion.

In this piece, Tom feels forced to leave home, leaving his tragically distressed and vulnerable sister behind with their overbearing and disturbed mother.

What I think you should do is pick some lines and just play around with it. I've made a few suggestions of my own at the end of the piece for you to try out. You don't have to do an American accent unless you want to or you are American.

Tom: I didn't go to the moon. I went much further—for time is the longest distance between two places. Not long after that I was fired for writing a poem on the lid of a shoebox. I left St. Louis. I descended the steps of the fire escape for a last time and followed, from then on, in my father's footsteps, attempting to find in motion what was lost in space. I traveled around a great deal. The cities swept about me like dead leaves, leaves that were brightly coloured but torn away from their branches. I would have stopped, but I was pursued by something. It always came upon me unawares, taking me altogether by surprise.

Perhaps it was a familiar bit of music. Perhaps it was only a piece of transparent glass. Perhaps I am walking along a street at night, in some strange city, before I have found companions. I pass the lighted window of a shop where perfume is sold. The window is filled with *pieces of coloured glass, tiny transparent bottles in delicate colours, like bits of a shattered rainbow. Then all at once my sister touches my shoulder. I turn around and look into her eyes. Oh Laura, Laura, I tried to leave you behind me, but I am more faithful than I intended to be! I reach for a cigarette, I cross the street, I run into the movies or a bar, I buy a drink, I speak to the nearest stranger—anything that can blow your candles out! For nowadays the world is lit by lightning!*

Blow out your candles, Laura – and so goodbye...

Things for you to try.

Take the sentence,

I would have stopped but I was pursued by something.

- Say the sentence really quickly and loud, but stop just before you say the last word. Stop for a count of three, then say *something* really quietly and with a rising pitch as if mystified.

- Say it with a dramatic pause just before *pursued*.

- Say it with a dramatic pause just after *pursued.*

- Say it all slowly.

- Say it emphasising *would*

It is quite an emotional poetic piece. What did you discover from the above exercise?

Now set up vocal experiments of your own using this and other sentences.

You are probably discovering that there is an infinite variety of choices and that each choice will make a slightly different meaning.

It's all part of the fun of discovering how your voice can change meaning. It can also change your character, or at least how your character is perceived by others. It's worth thinking about.

Chapter Eight

Diction and Projection and a few of their Friends

They sound like pretty old-fashioned words in the world of speech and drama. And in the real world too if it comes to that. But if your diction and projection are no good then frankly your speech is no good because people can't hear it very well. Simples.

What's the difference between the two?

Diction is all about speaking with clarity. So let's make this absolutely clear. You know yourself that when people mumble it's hard to understand them, that's kind of the definition of *mumble,* I guess. But what is it they are actually doing?

I'll tell you. As well as speaking quietly, they are not pronouncing **consonants** clearly.

If someone tells you that your diction is good, they mean you pronounce consonants precisely; it's not to do with accent or anything like that. Consonants are the hard edges of words. The river bank, if you like, while vowels are the river. Vowels are fluid. Consonants are more solid.

Consonants involve an interruption of the out-flowing voice by one of the following: lips, teeth, jaw, tongue, roof of the mouth.

Collectively, the organs of articulation.

The more firmly and securely you make the movement, the interruption, the clearer your speech will be, the easier to follow.

Choose one section of your speech, while rehearsing, and really focus on doing this. You want to get the balance right, of course, and not sound theatrically fake; a subtle yet definite exaggeration of the movement of the organs of articulation works wonders.

Try to really assimilate this and use it when speaking in public: you need to **articulate your consonants**. Implement this as you rehearse.

In this context vowels don't matter so much but consonants really matter a lot.

So when you practise your public speaking bear this in mind; try to be sure that your organs of articulation work harder, harder than they would in a normal conversation.

If this is something that you're just not used to doing, because maybe it sounds a little bit crazy and a little bit weird, then I would recommend you actually spend a little bit of time practising some of the consonant exercises that you find at the end of this chapter.

And if you don't think consonants are important in clarity of communication, here is a little interesting/amusing idea. Well, I think it's funny, anyway.

You could try saying the following sentence out loud but change all of the consonants and ask someone if they can understand what you are talking about.

This cheese smells unpleasant.

Your sentence would sound something like this:

Drig streed prefft uydweakaxy

Now repeat the same sentence but change all of the vowels and ask your patient friend, the one who is looking at you with raised eyebrows and bemused expression, the same question.

This time they should be able to understand you reasonably easily.

The second time it could have surfaced in this form:

Thas chaas smalls inplaisent.

The point of subjecting your long suffering friend to this is to make it clear to you how important consonants are in making your spoken words clear to an audience so, yes, it's all about being clear.

Now, I say it again, I know that some public speakers are good without any coaching, preparation or training whatsoever. But they would be better than they already are if they paid attention to all of the factors that go together to make up a good speech, a cracking, presentation, a brilliant talk.

And one of these factors is good diction.

So much for diction. I hope that has made it crystal clear.

Now for that other little devil, **projection**.

You may or may not have a microphone. Either way, your voice needs to be strong. As a public speaker you really need to command the arena. Otherwise, frankly, there's no point doing it.

You need to boss this space.

One of the ways of doing this is with your voice; we are not talking about bellowing like an old-fashioned drill Sergeant Major, we are talking about a powerful, authoritative voice that commands the attention of every single person in the room. It is a strong steady voice well supported by a smooth flow of breath with the exhaled breath being sustained right to the end of every sentence.

There is a huge difference between shouting and projecting. There is a reason why Aston Villa football supporters end up with sore throats after 90 minutes of watching the boys in claret and blue playing Birmingham City.

It's because they've been shouting. There's a reason why an opera singer performing in the open air arena of Verona and a beautiful starlit sky and being heard like cut crystal glass by 20,000 spectators, does not have a sore throat. It's because she's been projecting. Not shouting.

I'm not suggesting that you need to be a trained opera singer. That may take a while, maybe it will take a little bit too long, may not even be possible. I'm sure you're talented, but you may have limits.

I am suggesting that you do borrow some of the techniques used by opera singers, the

number one of which is you learn
intercostal diaphragmatic breathing.

The intercostals are the muscles between
your ribs; the diaphragm is a dome shaped
muscle at the base of your ribs and just
above the abdomen. You need to recruit
both of these to facilitate intercostal
diaphragmatic breathing.

The intercostal muscles are voluntary,
meaning that they are controlled by your
mind, whereas the diaphragm is involuntary
but it can be given a boost of power by the
use of the abdominal muscles.

Try to breathe, then, from your stomach.
Practise **breathing in** such that you feel the
air going right down to the bottom of the
lungs. You should feel the stomach moving
out. This is because, in effect, your brain
has told it to do that to bring the diaphragm
down. Do the opposite when you **breathe**

out, really feel the tummy moving in to help you with the effort. This makes the diaphragm work hard and push the air out with greater force.

As the air goes out forcefully, it takes your voice with it. To the back of the room. This is called diaphragmatic breathing.

Exercise to Develop Intercostal Diaphragmatic Breathing.

Try this: take a deep breath while putting one hand on your stomach and one hand at the base of the ribs. You can make yourself comfortable if you like and lie down. With cushions, of course.You will feel good movement in both places if you are breathing deeply, correctly for public speaking. Now breathe out slowly and smoothly.

You don't need to move your shoulders to breathe deeply, by the way.

Now say some words and focus on your breathing and on the sound travelling forwards. Imagine your voice as a tangible object that travels and think of it hitting a point on the ceiling. Use the ceiling as target practice.

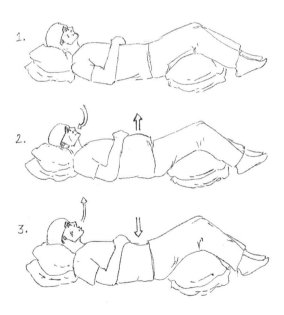

Incorporate this way of breathing and speaking.

You're not doing it properly if you feel/hear a rasping in the throat like you get when shouting.

I have considered offering my voice coaching sessions to my Aston Villa supporting friends. Not sure I'll get any takers.

Exercise for Diction

There are some famous tongue twisters. The point of this exercise is to say them carefully, accurately. And really concentrate on the consonants. And remember the way to concentrate on the consonants is to make your organs of articulation work hard.

Say them very slowly at first, not losing any of the consonants. Exaggerate the consonants a bit. Gradually speed up but don't turn it into a race. As you speed up concentrate more and more on not losing any of the clarity.

Peter Piper picked a peck of pickled peppers.

A peck of pickled peppers Peter Piper picked.

If Peter Piper picked a peck of pickled peppers?

Where's the peck of pickled peppers Peter Piper picked?

How much wood would a woodchuck chuck if a woodchuck could chuck wood?

He would chuck, he would, as much as he could, and chuck as much wood,

as a woodchuck would if a woodchuck could chuck wood.

She sells sea shells by the seashore.

Betty bought a bit of butter.

But the butter Betty bought was bitter.

so Betty bought a better butter,

and it was better than the butter Betty bought before.

Silly Sally swiftly shooed seven silly sheep.

The seven silly sheep Silly Sally shooed

Shilly-shallied south.

These sheep shouldn't sleep in a shack;

Sheep should sleep in a shed.

The sixth sick sheik's sixth sheep's sick.

Round the rough and rugged rock the ragged rascal rudely ran.

All I want is a proper cup of coffee,

Made in a proper copper coffee pot

I may be off my dot

But I want a cup of coffee

From a proper coffee pot.

Tin coffee pots and iron coffee pots

They're no use to me -

If I can't have a proper cup of coffee

In a proper copper coffee pot

I'll have a cup of tea.

Amidst the mists and coldest frosts,

With stoutest wrists and loudest boasts,

He thrusts his fists against the posts,

And still insists he sees the ghosts

I'd like a few more original tongue twisters. I didn't make these up myself, they're old ones. Can **you** make a few up? Send some in, if you can and I'll put them in the updated book with a credit.

They should focus on one particular consonant and if they are funny and rhyme so much the better. And you will get a mention the next book and a metaphorical pat on the back. Don't pinch your tongue twister from somewhere else. As if.

mike@or8.co.uk

Intonation, modulation and inflection.

These three little characters are so close in meaning they are practically brothers and sisters. Or cousins, at least. They are certainly good mates with projection and diction, living in the same neighbourhood.They all refer to the rise and fall of the voice combined with other vocal changes as to indicate the mood or meaning of the speaker.

Personally, I tend to think of inflection as being more focused on particular words as to highlight them in some way, whereas the others are a bit more general:

The way Kevin Curious used **rising inflection** when he said "yes?" made me think he wanted more information .

Maureen Manglefoot's **modulation** made her talk on fashionable footwear more interesting than it would have been.

Resonance

You know you can make your voice sound a bit more grand? To give it a sort of richness, texture and depth? To make it louder at the same time?

No? Well, you can.

This is called resonance. You are making the sound that comes from the vocal cords vibrate in the **vocal tract**. This is the whole area above the vocal cords and includes the throat, the mouth and the nasal cavity.

When your voice sounds resonant it adds a sense of importance to your words, a sense of real significance.

You can increase your resonance by doing this:

Exercise for Resonance

Hum. While humming, change the position of your jaw, tongue, lips, the soft palate (the back of the roof of the mouth) and then change the pitch and feel where the vibration is. Find the most resonating hum at each level, then you become aware of how you need to adjust your vocal tract to achieve that.

You can then apply different types of resonance to your script. Experiment with it and see what comes across well.

Chapter Nine

Movement and Gesture

Rhea is Nervous about Making Eye Contact

If you have the opportunity to move during your speech, then do so; and think of appropriate times for your movement and whether it would be better to moveup stage, downstage, stage right or stage left.

I'm referring here to the theatrical descriptions of stage movement. The back of the stage is called upstage and the front of the stage is called, yes, downstage. Stage right and stage left are from the perspective of the actor looking at the audience.

An easy way to remember this is that in the olden days, well, maybe in the 18th century, stages did actually slope a little bit down towards the audience. Sometimes they had very large numbers of people on stage at the same time and the actors at the back wanted to be seen by grandma in the audience. So they put them higher up.

That's a little bit of a digression but I think quite an interesting one.

<u>No Barriers</u>

If at all possible, avoid standing behind a table or podium. It may be that the people producing the event say that that's the way that it has to be done, maybe they have set up the lighting, microphones and everything in such a way that you don't have any choice.

But, as I say, if you can avoid it, do. This is really about you having an impact on the audience. Get out from behind the podium and talk to them. It makes them sit up and take notice. When you have a physical barrier in front of you it's like putting a psychological barrier up as well, and you have to work harder to overcome it.

Pacing

As with other aspects of your presentation, experiment with movement. Lots of speakers pace as they perform and audiences actually find this quite dynamic and interesting.

It doesn't detract and it actually can be helpful to the speaker because that kind of movement can help to disperse tension.

Irritating Movement

However, there are some types of movement that audiences do find annoying. And a lot of people do them:

- Rocking or swaying from one foot to the other. My colleague, Coral, calls this **the pirate walk**, as it looks like someone on a ship that's rocking.

- Repeatedly walking backwards and forwards, over and over and over.

- Jangling keys in pockets etc. In fact, lots of people do this or something similar. The fiddle unconsciously with something around about waist height. It might be the rim of their jacket, a tie, their cuffs etc, and they don't even know they are doing it. But it can look a bit daft. Watch out for it.

<u>Some Effective Moves</u>

Here's an interesting way of using movement:

If you are upstage and then you suddenly walk downstage, you look as if you might come off the stage at any moment to walk in amongst the audience. If, indeed you do that from time to time, your audience member thinks, "I'm definitely not going to switch off, then, I'm not going to start thinking about something else, this guy might talk to me and make the whole audience look at me."

And here's another one:

Find a line in your script that could be particularly moving or particularly dramatic. Highlight it. Then for the three or four sentences that immediately precede it, walk around the stage rapidly saying the lines quickly, then when you come to the sentence in question, stop dead still, pause. Then say the sentence in total stillness quietly but clearly.

Try it with this:

Exercise for Movement

> Say the first paragraph really fast and pacing about. Then at the end of the first paragraph, stop dead still and say the second paragraph slowly.
>
> *It's so easy to ignore poverty. For years I thought it was someone else's problem. Even though sometimes I*

gave a few coins to homeless people I never really thought about it deeply. Well, it's difficult, isn't it. We all have busy lives, we have deadlines and personal issues and so much going on and these people seem to live in another dimension. I never thought I would be like them.

On this exact day, this time last year, my world turned upside down.

Eye Contact

Look at the audience directly as much as you possibly can.

Use the "windscreen wiper" technique. Look in the direction of the audience on your left, at the audience directly in front of you, look in the direction of the audience on your right.

Keep doing this, varying the routine occasionally and obviously not always looking at the same person. Intersperse this with occasionally looking at the back and occasionally at the front.

This helps in making people feel that they are involved and that you really are trying to address them personally.

OH AND SMILE. People love it when you smile at them. Makes you look like a nice person. Maybe not too much, though. Especially if you are delivering bad news!

<u>Gesture</u>

Don't get too stressed about body language or movement.

It's important to have good posture and use gestures from time to time.

If you're worried about gestures then consciously apply them. Annotate your script, writing down when you use your hands to emphasise or illustrate a point.

It's usually best to restrict hand gestures to an imaginary box running down from the top of your head to the bottom of your tummy and extending not much wider than shoulders. Going outside of this may make you look a bit over excited. Someone may call the police.

Sometimes gestures are mini shorthand mimes of the thing being described; sometimes they indicate space or size by opening the hands wide apart or close together; sometimes they indicate a passage of time or that the situation is complex by rolling one hand over the other.

Sometimes absolutely no one knows what some hand gestures signify. It's just some mysterious connection between brains and hands. So, as I say, don't stress.

Here's a few that may signify:

Listing. Use your fingers to indicate numbers. Helps reinforce the number.

A Tiny Bit. As if you are holding a thin plate between fingers and thumb. For something that doesn't have to be taken too seriously or a small addition.

I'm Determined. Solid fist shaking for a very important point and the sheer force of your will. Maybe not accompanied by an irritated tone of voice unless you want to scare them or send for the police. Again.

Everything. For a big grand gesture, indicating the all inclusive nature of what you're saying, sweep your arms and hands widely left to right (or the other way!) This can also show that you are brushing something out of the way.

Steeple. With fingertips touching each other and maybe tapping. Makes you look wise, reflective. (Or a bit pompous and superior if you do it too much.)

Pointing. Can be bad if it looks accusatory, but depending on context and vocal tone, it can mean, "Hey, I just thought of this!" Or "This one's important."

Hey, I'm generous. Palms facing upwards and moving outwards in a sort of shrug.

This and That. For comparisons, setting as it were one thing on one side in a box and the other thing on the other side in another imaginary box.

Exercise for Movement and Voice

In this exercise I'm going to suggest that you experiment with both movement and voice. Again, it's from the world of drama. It's an emotional pace with lots of vocal range and effective movement.

Look at the following speech. It's taken from George Bernard Shaw's play, *St.Joan.*

Joan of Arc has been sentenced to life in prison, instead of burning at the stake, for leading soldiers into battle based on voices she has heard from Heaven. When she realizes that she is to be continually confined, she recants her confession and boldly addresses her inquisitors.

Joan: Yes, they told me you were fools, and that I was not to listen to your fine words nor trust to your charity. You promised me my life; but you lied. You think that life is nothing but not being stone dead. It is not the bread and water I fear: I can live on bread; when have I asked for more? It is no hardship to drink water if the water be clean. Bread has no sorrow for me, and water no affliction. But to shut me from the light of the sky and the sight of the fields and flowers; to chain my feet so that I can never again ride with the soldiers no climb the hills; to make me breathe foul damp darkness, and keep from me everything that brings me back to the love of God when your wickedness and foolishness tempt me to hate Him: all this is worse than the furnace in the Bible that was heated seven Emes. I could drag about in a skirt; I could let the banners and the trumpets and the knights and soldiers pass me and leave me behind as they leave the other women, if only I could sEll hear the wind in the trees, the larks in the sunshine, the young lambs crying through the healthy frost, and the blessed, blessed church bells that send my angel voices floating to me on the wind. But without these things I cannot live; and by your wanting to take them away from me, or from any *human creature, I know that your counsel is of the devil, and that mine is of God.*

What you could do is get a pencil and annotate it according to your different ideas. So for example, take the sentences,

You promised me my life; but you lied. you think that life is nothing but not being stone dead.

What you could do is start that first sentence off fairly quietly and slowly, *you promised me...* and build up pace, pitch and volume to reach a climax at the end of the sentence. You could walk powerfully downstage whilst saying this, then stop dead and give a dramatic pause before turning round silently, walking upstage then turning back to face the audience to say in a low but well projected whisper, *but you* (pause) *lied.*

Now, to be honest, those were just random thoughts about how to deliver it. Why don't you pick those same lines and do something completely different? Then experiment with other parts of the speech or, indeed all of it.

When you work like this, don't be afraid to go over the top, it can actually be helpful in freeing you from inhibitions. You can calm it down and be more realistic any time you like.

This is what you might call an external way of approaching the piece, by which I mean looking at the body and voice without necessarily feeling the feelings that the character would be experiencing . And this can work to actually stimulate the feelings. Things are working outside in as it were.

I haven't given you a dramatic script because I want you to be an actor. It's so you get used to the idea of using your voice and the space available to you so that you can gain dramatic effects with your speech.

Chapter Ten

The Public Speaker as an Actor

215

What Comes Naturally?

This can be a little bit controversial as some people think that if you start using an actor's techniques then you are taking away from the sincerity of your performance.

We are back to the Sophists again.

I remember once I was interested in working as a public speaking coach with a private company whose name I won't mention, well, I can't remember it actually, but it was something like, *Be a Naturally Good Speaker*, and I phoned them to ask what the score was.

The guy on the phone was quite amenable until he said to me, "Tell me a little bit about your philosophy for coaching people in public speaking," and I replied that I was coming from a background of drama teaching and I thought that an actor's skills were very important as a public speaker.

He told me in no uncertain terms that he and his colleagues believe the exact opposite of that, they thought it was absolutely wrong to try to coach normal people to become actors, "You can't train your average person to be a Meryl Streep. We think that whole approach is just baloney."

Only he didn't say baloney.

Then he said people just have to be themselves.

So the conversation ended there, really. A bit rude I thought.

I don't think the approach is baloney or any other kind of sausage. I think the world of acting can provide enormous support to a public speaker. Many of the technical skills that I refer to in this book, like voice and movement, are totally relevant to the world of public speaking.

And there is another way in which we can draw on this field.

It's a psychological approach to acting that we can apply to public speaking. And I offer this to you as a way of thinking about the whole business.

Stanislavski

First I need to tell you about a guy called Konstantin Stanislavski. In the late 19th and early 20th century, Stanislavski worked out a system of actor training. He was an actor himself and a theatre director he set up his own theatre company called the Moscow Art Theatre.

In Moscow.

He wanted the actors who performed in his company to act very realistically. I know that doesn't sound like such a big deal, but it was back then; most performances then were over the top, melodramatic. They didn't seem much like real life at all.

Stanislavski wanted to change all of this and get realism or naturalism, as it's more accurately called, onto the stage. But he found that it wasn't as easy as all that.

When he acted himself, which he still did from time to time, he found that sometimes his performances were tremendous, inspired and terrific; other times they were pretty much rubbish. And so he dedicated himself to trying to work out a method that would make his performances great every single time.

His productions would then be true to life.

Some years and a lot of blood, sweat and tears later, he came up with what is often called the Stanislavski System. Sometimes it's called Method Acting and various theatrical practitioners have amended, changed it and added to it over the years.

I'm going to sum up many years of Stan's work and thousands of pages of print in a few sentences here. Cheeky of me, really.

The system says you have to think yourself into the role of the part that you are playing. You have to imagine that you could be that person and you have to think how you would behave if you were in their situation.

Then you can live the part.

So in order to do this you think about time that you felt like that character; you try to make those feelings feel fresh and new in yourself and then, when you're playing the part, you apply those feelings to the performance and you recreate them.

However, you don't take your eye off the ball, you remember at all times that you are performing, so you have a dual perspective. Part of you thinks that you really are this character and the other part of you knows that you are absolutely not that character.

If this sounds a little odd, a little bit strange and a little bit like, well, mind teasing, I would say: think about a child playing *let's pretend*. They can be so completely and utterly immersed in their play that they totally believe the fictional reality they've created for themselves. And yet as soon as mummy says it's teatime, the child drops Paddington Bear on the gravel instantly and runs in to gobble down the biscuits.

Well, the dual perspective is like that.

There we are, a lifetime's work of genius summed up in a150 words (count them*) by a Drama Teacher.

What's the relevance of this to your approach to public speaking?

I'll tell you.

You imagine that the speech that you've got ahead of you is a role in a play, and is going to be performed by an actor. That actor is you. You are going to be playing a part. The "character" has the same name as you and looks like you, but it's a version of you. A version of you that is confident and full of conviction; the message that is being conveyed is hugely important and the character believes in it massively.

The character that you're playing is never nervous and is a great public speaker.

Now think yourself into this role. Take a few quiet moments and remember a time when you have felt very confident. Start to really refresh those memories, start to feel them and think: where was I when I was so confident, what did it feel like?

How good does that feel now?

Now take a look at your script and bring those feelings of self confidence and enthusiasm and make them breathe life to this script in front of you. Keep that self-confidence going as you perform the speech.

Now think of a time when you felt very strongly that the message that you needed to speak, was very very important to you.

Refresh those memories within your mind, within your heart.

Make it happen again, then take those feelings to your script and with your confidence and your convictions perform the speech like that.

Another aspect to this technique which by the way is called, Emotion Memory, is to think of another person whom you have seen with these characteristics.

The qualities of self confidence and conviction.

Imagine what it must've felt to be that person when they were speaking if they were on the stage. What would it be like to be so in control of an audience to feel yourself into their spirit?

Make those feelings live fresh for you and then rehearse with your script bringing those feelings to overlay the ones you've already put there.

You are creating an invincibility cloak.

Put on the metaphorical cloak of this character when your rehearsals start to get close to the actual performance.

Put it on the cloak during the actual performance and use it as a shield.

Another mixed metaphor for you. A mixed metaphor, in case you don't know, is when you get two or more metaphorical comparisons that just don't go together. If you did know, then please unread the last sentence. And this one.

*I lied about the word count.

Chapter Eleven

Visual Aids

The Only Visual Aids Sana Needs

<u>The Clue is in the Words.</u>

What do you think is the key word in the title of this book?

Well, it's not *how,* is it?

The key word in the title of this book is *speaking.* The skill that you are developing is that of creating and delivering brilliant words; and **visual aids are there to support you not to supplant you.**

Visual aids are great if they help the audience to engage with your speech.

In this chapter, when I refer to slides I mean any images or words displayed. So in Speech and Drama exams it's usually pictures on cards, in business it's usually Powerpoint slides.

The purpose of visual aids is something you need to think about. They should be:

- to explain something that's difficult

- to add an extra element to the explanation by presenting the information differently. This might be called Show <u>and</u> Tell.

- And if possible to delight the eyes of the audience

It's a bad idea to use bullet points or at least too many bullet points and it's a bad idea to overload any one slide with too much information.

You don't want people staring at the screen trying to figure it out.

I was once examining a student in public speaking whose visual aids were so complex, I hadn't got a clue what he was on about.

I remember it clearly. He was telling me about a video game that he loved so much. He had a series of slides that were all highly convoluted flow charts of the different courses of action a player could take and the consequences of taking different decisions.

As he explained - and I use the word lightly - he used a lot of subject specific vocabulary. He may as well have been speaking an ancient and long dead language as far as I was concerned. And demonstrating it with Egyptian hieroglyphics.

And it was a shame because he obviously loved the topic.

But I had no idea what he was talking about.

The slides are there to illustrate, simplify, reinforce a point, or provide visual evidence. They are not there as a crutch.

And they mustn't be a distraction.

At any one point, the audience is taking in what is in the visual aid <u>or</u> they are listening to your words. They are not doing both at the same time.

The very worst presentations are when someone simply reads slides out. I mean, what's the point? Slides or any visual aids with words on them should be abbreviated so you are forced to read round the content. It makes it much more engaging. And it means the audience doesn't know what you are going to say before you have said it, leaving them impatient for the next bit.

It's also very good to use animation in slides; it keeps things dynamic but the eye always moves to a moving object, so don't overdo it, you want their eyes on you.

Interesting Slides*

Sometimes it's good to think about the timing of when to reveal an image. If your slide contains an idea or image you want to reveal to the audience as a surprise or revelation then, you don't want that slide to be visible to the audience too soon. You don't want to pre-empt yourself.

I really liked it in one of my student's recent speeches, he talks about global warming. He asks the audience what is to blame and holds up a series of Images. He shows them factories billowing out smoke and asks "This?"; then a traffic jam, "This?", then he says "This?" and shows them an image of a cow, grazing in a field.

He goes on to talk about how the release of methane from cows as they pass wind is a significant contributor to the problem and argues for the consumption of much less meat.

The point I'm making here is that if the cow had been visible all the time, it would have lost its impact.

A very common mistake is for speakers to talk to the slides and not to the audience.

The last thing you want to do is have your back to the audience while looking at the slides.

Finally be prepared to do your presentation without your slides. We have all seen people struggling and looking embarrassed and flustered because the technology has let them down.

*its bad when you need to explain a joke. But maybe it's necessary. I didn't know these kind of shoes are called slides.

Chapter Twelve

How to Handle Those Nerves

Speaking on Stage make you want to... SCREAM?

Anya Goes All Munch

One Thing You Must Do

The One Thing You Must Do: Prepare

Prepare, prepare, prepare.

I guess that's three things..?

It's a little bit dull, as it's not a magic wand or a silver bullet, but preparation is way and beyond more important than all the rest.

Make sure that you know exactly what you are going to say. And while it's better not to look at note cards or at the screen, make sure you have a bullet point list in your pocket in case you "dry." When an actor says they have dried, they mean that when performing their mind just goes completely blank. And the more they try to remember their words, the harder it gets to do so.

A few points about cue cards.

Number your cards clearly in case you drop them. Just write a few key words on them to remind you of different sections of your speech. IN BIG CAPITALS: You don't want to be squinting at them when you are already under pressure.

They are great if you get stuck, but they become a problem if you look at them too much. I've seen it loads of times when the speaker looks at their cards almost all of the time, even when they're not actually reading anything off them. The cards have become a way of avoiding eye contact with the audience. Then the speaker doesn't communicate very well and a lot of the power of the speech has gone.

Also, what I see a lot is a presenter starting to look down at the next cue card before they have finished their point. They often combine this with dropping their voice. This,

I'm sorry to say it, is really rubbish. You are throwing lines away.

Then Rehearse. Till you are blue in the face. Or indigo. Keep at it.

What do do if you Dry

When you dry, you find yourself in an unpleasant place. Not as unpleasant as some areas of the city I live in. And probably not as unpleasant as some areas in your city or village or backwater, but definitely not a nice place.

It's a bleak state of mind and body.

You have no clue what you are supposed to say next. And people are staring at you expectantly. Their staring changes to embarrassment which makes it worse. Your throat goes dry and panic sets in. Just when you need a cool head you've got a rattled brain and a sense of fear overcoming you.

Now there is no solid reason for this fear; you're not in a Formula One car driving 190 miles an hour about to shoot off the road, you're just a person who is looking a bit silly.

But getting it into a sense of proportion is not on the cards when you dry.

What is on the cards, luckily, are bullet points, with a very clear list of everything you have to say in the right order and summarised succinctly. You have this even if you are using a teleprompter and slides.

Then attempting to look like Mr or Miss or Mrs or Ms Cool, you just calmly take the notes out of your pocket, acting like you had planned to do that all along.

If you have rehearsed a lot, you'll soon pick up the thread. And dryness vanishes like summer dew.

Another thing you can do if you dry, provided you feel up to it: Laugh it off.

This really depends on the context and on how you are feeling, but sometimes it actually works very powerfully in your favour if you can say, "Do you know, I've completely forgotten where I was."

You can even ask the audience what was the last thing you said. By doing this with no sign of fear, you have actually built up your ethos (see rhetoric) and shown how confident you are.

Or ask the audience a question. If you're confident enough. It takes the focus and pressure off you and puts a bit of that same focus and pressure on the audience. As they respond, it gives you thinking time. It has other benefits too, increasing audience engagement.

Remember, though, to stay in charge.

Practise the piece at home, over and over again in the privacy of your own solitude. Visualise yourself being great.

Do this at least five times without stopping. When you get to the actual performance, say to yourself:

Look, I've done this five times without any hitches. So why should this be any different?

Note. It *could* be different if technology lets you down. So never, ever rely on tech. I've seen it too often and so quite possibly have you. A speaker who turns up with a presentation all on slides think the slides are going to be wonderful and think the slides are going to do the work for them and their technology breaks down.

And so does the speaker. Disaster.

Remember the audience has come to see you are you, not to see PowerPoint. They can do that any time.

Six Things You Could Do.

1. Act.

Imagine it's an acting performance. As outlined in the previous chapter.

This is not for everyone. Some people like a bit of role play, some people hate it. But for absolute sure, it works for some people.

When I was a drama teacher in a school, I had one student who I knew was a really good actor, been in lots of shows and was really good in drama classes. And he came up to me one day and said he was so worried about doing a presentation to the school that he had been asked to do by a history teacher because he was very knowledgeable on the Battle of Hastings.

He told me he didn't want to let the teacher down but he was scared of doing a presentation.

I said to him why don't you just pretend that you are acting a part? And do you know, he instantly, and I mean, instantly, said "Oh, yeah, great, yeah, I'll do that."

The performance he gave didn't look like a performance, just came across as a very good presentation. He was acting a character very much like him who happened to be good at presenting and thought of it as if he was in a play.

So just play pretend.

Pretend it's not you, but it is a version of you. It's you being very confident, competent and friendly. It's a character. You've learned the script and you're now going to perform it. This is my personal favourite and I've seen it work for lots of people, a little bit like the elusive silver bullet.

2. It's about the Message.

Remember the importance of your topic.

Keep it front of mind that you really want the audience to know this. Keep thinking of the audience and what they are going to get out of this. Focus on them, not on yourself.

It's not about you, it's about them.

And speaking of the audience, please remember that they want you to be good.

They are on your side (usually) and they are decent people with feelings, empathy and a sense of humour.

This relates to the old idea, put about by some, that you should imagine your audience naked. I don't recommend this attitude but it comes from the idea that you should not be over respectful of the people in front of you. They are mere flesh and blood like the rest of us.

3.Perspective.

Try putting the whole thing in perspective.

No one is going to die if you give a bad presentation. Even if it's rubbish you will survive. Maybe compare this experience with something much worse that has happened to you: If I survived that, I can survive this.

Old fashioned self-control.

You can personify and manage the voice in your head that tells you to be scared.

Tell that nagging voice to go away. Just tell it. Mentally say, "I'm not going to be nervous, you naughty little voice, leave me alone, I'll be great"

Whenever you feel it rearing its ugly little head, tell it to go away. If it helps, visualise the nervous voice as a person, make it, in your mind's eye, gradually smaller and paler as it shrinks away and disappears.

4. Use Positive Body Language.

Try this right now. If you are on your own. You may look a bit weird otherwise.

Sit in a chair. Look at the space in front of you and imagine yourself standing there. Imagine what your stance and facial expression would be like if you were feeling really confident. Visualise this as vividly as possible for several seconds. Then stand up into that space and adopt that exact stance.

You should find it feels great. You actually feel like that confident person.

So we know that if we feel good in our minds that it tends to show in our body and face; well, it often works the other way too.

When you get on the stage to present and when you are rehearsing, use this technique. Be physically big, smile, use open gestures and body language.

5. It's not that Bad

Compare your fear to fear of something much worse (without getting all hysterical.)

This can be a neat and effective way of managing your worries. Think of something terrifying that you or someone you know has experienced, then compare it with what you are about to do. No-one is going to die if you give a poor speech.

6. Be Ahead of Time

Get to the venue early. You've really got to do this. Practise on the stage. This will help you immensely in controlling your nerves.

Walk around the arena and imagine people sitting right at the back. Remember, this is your space. Speak to the people right at the back. If they can hear and see you clearly, then so can everyone else.

Make Sure it's a Good Delivery

Krishna is Bowled Over by this Book

For the last five or six run throughs, don't look at the script.

At this stage, when you are rehearsing without holding or looking at the script, the quality of your performance dips a bit as you struggle to remember the words.

Don't give up the attempt to do it from memory. Keep at memorising in between dry runs. You will get there.

But...

if you try to give a speech from memory and you haven't properly memorised it, you are in trouble. And you would have been better off sticking to referring to bullet points. But because by now you have done so much work on your presentation it's usually pretty easy to memorise.

Keep at it til the words are second nature.

In the final stages of rehearsal you really need to put your whole heart and soul into delivering the piece with passion, even if you don't get the words exactly right.

You're concentrating now on your performance and communicating your ideas and the truth of the material.

Really valuable too, is to **time your rehearsals,** your run throughs. Event organisers and examiners are working to a schedule. They want the timing of your piece right. The speed you deliver the piece in rehearsals needs to be the desired time of the final performance.

If you can, have the last rehearsal at the venue.

And fully check it out before you start.

Particularly focus on the perimeter of your performance area, the outer limits. Your voice and your personality must at the very least reach these areas and you must boss this space.

When you get really close to performance, the words of your script should be so internalised that muscle memory could pretty much do this piece without you.

But

- Check any equipment/props are in place and working.

- You should have emergency "if-memory-fails-notes." Make sure you know where they are.

- **Be aware that the places where presenters often lose track are at linking sections** or discourse markers, so make a point of trying to really focus on these during rehearsals.

Now. Get on Stage. And attack.

Try to live in the moment. Focus on the importance of your message and on your real desire to communicate it effectively to this audience, in this place, at this time.

Your complete and utter familiarity with the material should allow you a little bit of flexibility with it. So if, for example, something unexpected happens in the arena, you can respond to it and perhaps even interweave it with the message of your material.

And there might be a little bit of interaction with the audience. Maybe this is something that you've planned before, or it might just happen spontaneously in reaction to something. This is great and can be highly effective, reminding people of the live nature of the event and giving them a sense that almost anything could happen. It adds to the excitement and engagement.

But just remember, as well, that audience interaction can be a double edged sword. You are the one in control. If you invite audience responses, don't let them get carried away, don't let them take the initiative from you so that it becomes their show and not yours.

And it really is **your** show.

Chapter Fourteen

Where to Develop Your Skills

If I were a rugby player, which thank the lord I'm not, sir, then I wouldn't simply play games, competitive games, I would also have practice games.

These would be of course opportunities to hone my skills to get better at being a flanker or a kicker or a hooker or whatever else rugby players strive to become.

Not being a rugby player but fancying myself as something of a good public speaker, I also look for opportunities to practise, to have a practice game

There aren't too many opportunities for practice games in the public speaking malarkey but there are some.

Apart from those opportunities given to you from time to time by your English teacher, try to find out if you can get involved in a debate.

The Formal Debate

What happens in a formal debate is that you have two teams and they are given a topic or, in debating parlance, a motion. One side has to argue in favour of the motion and the other side has to argue against it.

You have a real audience who listens and at the end they vote on who they believe has won the argument.

Very often if you're in a debate you will be arguing against something that you don't actually believe in; the proverbial turkey voting for Christmas, if you see what I mean.

The very fact that you are arguing for something that you may not believe in, is a good thing because it means that you just concentrate on how to create a good case and you focus on how to present that case.

In other words, you are practising being a public speaker without getting too emotionally involved in the topic. Well of course you may actually get emotionally involved if it is something that you really strongly feel about but it's equally likely that you won't give two hoots.

You're really just practising being a public speaker.

If you want to look into the career histories of many of our most successful politicians and indeed barristers you will pretty much for sure find out that in their youth they took part in formal debates.

If there isn't a club where you are, why not set one up yourself? There's lots of people out there who'd like to give it a go. Or if you're in school, nag your English teacher.

Speech and Drama Exams

Another thing you could do is get private lessons from a Speech and Drama teacher.

They will coach you and enter you for a graded exam.

There are five Speech and Drama examining boards in the United Kingdom, you can take an exam with them in the UK or elsewhere in the world.

It's really not very much like a GCSE exam or an A-level exam or an IB for that matter. Speech and Drama exams are more like the kind of thing you would expect for a dance exam or a musical instrument exam.

Typically you prepare one, two or sometimes three speeches, you learn then, and you learn some theory, you learn how to deliver these speeches from memory. For some exam boards and at some grades you also have to do an impromptu speech and you are given about 15 minutes to plan what you are going to say.

Your teacher will book you in for an exam and then you get an appointment card telling you where and when to go and be examined.

When you get to the exam you will be asked to go into the exam room at the appointed time where you will find an examiner sitting behind a desk. They ask you to perform your speeches, they take a little while to mark your pieces and then they ask you to sit down and they ask you questions about the theory.

A Speech and Drama exam typically takes around 20 minutes, it can be a bit shorter for younger students and it can be up to 10 minutes longer for older students.

Exams are graded and typically start at grade 1 and go up to grade 8 but you need to check individual boards for details. The demands on the candidate get greater as you go up through the grades, as you would expect.

The main exam boards in the United Kingdom are: English Speaking Board (ESB), London Academy of Music and Dramatic Art (LAMDA), London College of Music (LCM), New Era Academy (NEA), Trinity College, and Victoria.

Chapter Fifteen

Sample Speeches

In this section I'm going to show you some of the speeches made by my own students in recent years. So if you're doing a speech exam, they may give you some idea of the kind of material you can use. They might stimulate your thoughts.

I've been thinking about how to describe and give a title to this and I've come up with Sample Speeches.

Sheer Genius.

I've been lucky enough to have coached hundreds, I mean, literally, hundreds of students in public speaking. It's a great creative process that both I and the students enjoy. I just give you a little bit of an outline of how we arrived at the speeches that follow.

The speeches are not perfect, all of the students and I would agree that they could probably be incrementally improved with further work. But these are real speeches created and developed with care and devotion. To a deadline. And in the exam they were all presented very professionally.

And, as another disclaimer, all teachers work differently and I'm not putting forward my approach as the best or only way of doing things.

Most of these speeches were prepared following the Lamda Speaking in Public Syllabus. Students at grades above grade 4 have to prepare and present two speeches of up to four minutes length. The speeches have to be original. One of the speeches has to be from a list of topics or on a certain theme, the other is free choice. They may use note cards but mustn't read the speech out. There has to be an imagined audience which they state at the start of the exam. They also have to give an impromptu speech at higher grades having been given a list of three to choose from fifteen minutes before the exam.

Students and I start off discussing what the syllabus demands from the speeches.

Then we have to find a suitable topic. Not just suitable for the syllabus but for the student. It has to be something they find exciting. It has to be something they really feel strongly that they want to do. Otherwise it's just not fun.

So it has to capture the imagination in some way. This does not necessarily mean that they believe in the argument that they are deploying, although that is often the case, rather it means that the idea of presenting this particular subject excites them regardless of whether it ties in with a personal belief.

Finding the right subject for a speech can take a long time. But it's worth it. Both the student and I are motivated when we have found something exciting and challenging.

There then follows further talk as we decide on the best way to approach it. I obviously have my input as a teacher but it's important for me that the student feels that it is their work. I make numerous suggestions and many are rejected by the student who often has better ideas of her own. Some of my ideas they agree with, but modify them.

Although there is a lot of talk in the early stages, there has to be practical work too. From the start it's important to get the student on their feet and performing. This is especially necessary with a more reserved student.

If it were left too long it could become an insurmountable mental block.

Most of the youngsters I teach tend to come from a science/maths type background. I don't know why but they do. And for some of these youngsters the idea of doing something like standing up and, as it were, pretending, is a bit alien. Not to all of them, of course, but a lot.

Just last week a former student came online when I was teaching his younger brother - this was written during lockdown - to tell me that he had just produced a play at Bristol University where he is studying Dentistry. He said he would never have done anything like produce a play if it hadn't been for his lessons with me. Nice.

So I get them to do something practical really early on. If they are really shy I take it very easy and stress that it's only going to be brief and they don't even have to be any good. No judgement.

Typically I will get them to pretend they are making an entrance on stage. I ask them to walk from the side of the room to "centre stage" with a very confident gait, bordering on a swagger, and to say in a good strong clear voice, "Good Morning, ladies and gentlemen."

That's usually enough to break the ice. The progress in terms of willingness to perform is pretty rapid after this, when they realise nothing bad is going to happen and actually it feels great.

We always spend the longest time deciding on the hook. When you've got the hook, you're off.

We move slowly towards a script through a process of discussion and experimentation. I will say things like "Do you think this bit is too strident, or is it hitting the right note?"

Often we can't decide the answer to a question like that so we try it out. Maybe I will perform the line myself in two or three different ways so they can make a judgement. More often they try it out themselves and we almost always agree on which sounds the best. You can just tell.

As more and more ideas come along, we start to think about the structure and whether or not we can fit all the material into the structure outlined in this book.

It's not always the case that it fits neatly into the structure but it's a living thing evolving in front of us. It's our baby and babies don't always do what you expect.

I can honestly say that when these speeches were performed, they were all delivered with passion and a high level of technical skill.

Another thing that makes teaching public speaking so enjoyable is the way you get to explore different subjects. Although, as I said, I have taught hundreds of students, each speech is unique in content and delivery. It's wonderful finding out about all the topics my students explore. It's life-enriching.

The Speeches

I haven't been able to include all of the speeches my students have presented; that would need a few volumes. So I've just picked a few from those scholars I'm still working with and who happen to have their speeches saved on computer.

Where you see bold type in brackets and underlined, that's me highlighting things you may care to notice. It wasn't on the student's copy.

My students tend to be academic but when writing their speeches, they often haven't bothered with accurate punctuation or spelling. This is fine because originally these pieces were meant for their eyes only. You're looking at working documents. If they had been writing essays they would have got it right, easily. But you may remember my earlier point about not worrying too much about this. The point of your script is that it's not going to be read by others, it's going to be performed by you. So forget SPAG. (Spelling, Punctuation and Grammar, for you non-school students.)

This first speech was constructed and delivered by Krishna, he was 15 at the time. All of the speeches were written and presented by students in their teens.

He had to compose and present a speech from a list of words. He chose the word, Competitions.

Krishna's Speech: Competitions.

Moon River wider than a mile. Krishna began his speech singing, very loudly and very badly. If that isn't a hook to grab attention, I don't know what is.)

I'm sorry, I'm sorry, that's hurting your ears, it's painful, I'll stop.

However, I sang that live on stage in front of millions of people on TV on the singing contest, The Voice. Of course, I didn't win, and people laughed at me.

However, did it destroy my self confidence? No. Did it kill me? Obviously not. Did I learn from it? Hell yeah! **(Series of rhetorical questions)**

Hello, my name is Krishna **(Inroduction)**

And I am going 2 to talk about why competitions are fun, and also so vital to everyday life. I bring this point up now because there is a growing move from Society from certain quarters to remove competitions as if they were evil and unnatural. As ifthey are wrong.

Today I am going to talk about: How competitions are found naturally, and in day to day jobs, How competitions make entertainment really interesting, And how competitions make us learn a lot. (Overview)

(Three main Points coming up)

Firstly, (Discourse Marker) Competitions are found naturally. For example, they are found in evolution. We've all heard about the survival of the fittest in which the organism best adapted to particular conditions survive and reproduce.

Competitions are also found naturally in love where animals compete to find a mate. Clearly competitions are present in all organisms, not just humans.

Furthermore, competitions are found between businesses in which each business tries to do better than the other to get more profit By having USPS so that people buy from their particular business. Competitions are also present in jobs because if the company you work for finds somebody better than you to do the job then you may be replaced. There is competition between people when applying for the job in interviews too as a company may only pick 1 out of a handful of people. Even before you are an adult you may have to compete for a university seat by having the best application. Competitions are evidently everywhere.

 Secondly, (DM) life Would Be Boring without competitions. for example Sport what would have no meaning at all had there been no competition.   imagine going to the stadium to watch Manchester City vs Aston Villa. how boring would it be if nobody cared what the end score would be? In fact Sports probably wouldn't have even existed without competitions as nobody would have been enthusiastic about it. Also, so many TV shows have competitions. for example The Apprentice and The Great British Bake Off are only interesting to watch because of the competition.

Thirdly, (DM) we can learn from competitions. This is because when you lose you can realise why you didn't win from which you can learn, and do better next time. And the people who lose are not really losers Until they give up. And competitions are so thrilling and exciting too!

We see competitions in schools, within schools, in countries, between countries, in sports competitions, in lotteries ,in love and evolution, in music competitions ,in beauty competitions...hoo...this is exhausting...(he paused and took a deep breath, having delivered this crazy long speech with ever increasing pace and power)

It is present in The Great British Bake Off, The Apprentice, Strictly Come Dancing, Love Island, in jobs in manufacturing products, within political parties ,between political parties and in discoveries. and I haven't even started, so I won't.

<u>(Amusing upbeat finish)</u>

To conclude and I'm talking to those people who would remove competitions, if it was possible, you would be taking away the fun from life.

Including letting you guys listen to me singing Moon River. And I know how much you love that!

<u>Reflections on Krishna's Speech</u>

Well,obviously, I like it. I always enjoy the work these guys produce. I really do. Each speech is a little joy in its own right. Well, now I've said that, I don't need to say it for all of the others. But it's true for all of them.

We were aiming for a lighter touch with this piece. In the exam the students have to deliver two speeches. I tend to suggest that one of the two is fairly serious in content and style and that the other is a bit more fun. In the exam itself I always suggest that the more serious of the two is delivered first. This lets the examiner know that you can do a formal weighty piece. Then you do something with more character and maybe some humorous flourishes.

So what about the content? You'll notice that Krishna started off singing. And boy, did he attack it. He really let rip. And it was unpleasant to listen to. He had to have some guts to do this. Because he knew it would make him look silly. But he also knew it would wake up the examiner if he had had a long day examining. Or if he hadn't. It would make the examiner think, "Well, this isn't going to be dull." And it created a sense of intrigue: "Is this guy serious?"

Then of course it tied in with what he was going to go on to say.

Of course, it wasn't true that he had appeared on *The Voice*. And this brings us to the question of whether or not things you say in a public speaking examination have to be true. I take the view that a fictional situation has been created by the syllabus because you have to state an imagined audience. Therefore, you, in your imagined situation respond, sort of in character. However, I always make it really clear to the candidate that the situation must be such that it could be a real speech in a real situation. This is not an Acting Examination.

The next speech is by Rhea.This was for her Grade 8 exam. At Grade 8, students have to present a political/cultural issue in one of their speeches. She decided she wanted to do something strong and forceful and highly subjective. The views in the speech are not necessarily her own.

Rhea's Speech: The NHS

in Chicago, USA in 2019. A, happy young woman- Freida, who was a primary school teacher and also herself had a young girl was diagnosed with a life-threatening metastatic cancer-needing multiple chemotherapy sessions to treat.as Unfortunately freida was underins Hook opening uses an emotive story. Pathos)

ured by her insurance company, her husband contacting other companies BUT STILL they were unable to reach the money needed for treatment.The treatment she received was third-rate and unprofessional. Eventually, she lost her fight with life and her young daughter grew up without a mother.

This could never happen in the Uk ,could it, with our NHS, **(Dramatic Pause)**or could it ?**(DP)**

BELIeve it or not , we are going to be finding more and more cases like this more and more often , we'll be finding them everywhere due to the Conservatives obsession with privatisation.

I'm Rhea, the Shadow Secretary for health and today I'm going to tell you of a deadly danger we face. **(Intro and credentials)**

we are already seeing a gradual increase in the amount of NHS budget going to large private firms such as Virgin Care, Care UK and Bupa.

The BMA reports that every year for the past five years, the amount of money spent by the NHS England on healthcare that is actually provided by the independent sector has increased, with the current yearly total at almost £7bn, totalling 6.3% of the total NHS budget

We CANT (Rhea gives herself capitals to remind her where to emphasise)afford to let the Tories rip apart the NHS like this. Private Healthcare is a plague to our society as it without a doubtbenefits the wealthy. Because of courseOnly those with wealth can access private healthcare,

lets just think about what some of these problems this country has   WE HAVE AGINING POPULATION , 27 percent of the population are over 65 so we are gonna need more bed , we gonna need more doctorswe gonna need more equipment.to say that the answer to this is privitisation???(This is her way of reminding herself to use rising inflection at a question)Is rdiciulous

284

We need to provide more state care to solve these problems, and for one thing what makes you think that private companies can manage this better?Ill tell you something, if private companies stop making money, gueess what - they'll stop providing the service!!!1! (For emphasis obvs.You wouldn't do this in an essay)Then where are we?? And then what will happen to the patients who were promised their care?

Again some people think that because there are so many private companies, and that they are all in competition with each other so of course they would provide the best possible service? But NO THAT IS NOT NECESSARILY SO

ALL this compeitition means that some of them WILL BE immoral in the way that they find the drugs that they sell to us ,just to keep the prices down, this is going to mean that sometimes(don't think this can't happen because it could) THOSE DRUGS WILL NOT BE thoroughly properly testedEvery single year in the United States, more than 200,000 (Logos)people die due to some kind of prescription drug

The only way to protect our NHS is to bin the Tory privatisation rules and restore a public NHS for all."

I would like to remind you of the words of the founder of the nhs - aneurin bevan WHO SAID ,"No society can legitimately call itself civilised if a sick person is denied medical care because of a lack of means".(quoting a politician of almost saint-like reputation lends the speaker some of his Ethos)

-----We don't want there to be people experiencing the same thing that freida went through. WE dont want your elderly father whose dying of cancer to be worried about selling his own house, WE DO NOT WANT PRIVITISATIO (strong finish)

Reflections on Rhea's Speech

It's powerful. Rhea and I talked about this for a long time. She said she wanted to do something potent. We discussed,among other things, the whole NHS issue surrounding state/private ownership and management. The subject was pertinent because we were in the middle of the Covid 19:outbreak.

We talked about whether to take an impartial view or to be partisan. Rhea decided that taking a strong line would enable her to give the sort of dramatic presentation she wanted.

The Next Speech is by Lasa.

Lasa was 11 at the time she made this speech. I can't remember what grade she was taking but it was when you had to speak about a personal interest.

Lasa's Speech:Reading.

Can you imagine eating a piece of cheese? Lovely, right? What about eating a piece of cheese, which has been on a playground floor for days. Maybe months. According to some children, even years. When you lift up that cheese and finish every last bit of it.(Put hand over mouth and gulp)(stage direction to herself) It was disgusting. Though, I loved... (pause) reading it! You thought I was going to say eating it. I would never do that. That was an incident from Diary of a wimpy kid by Jeff Kinney. My personal interest is reading and that is what I am going to be talking about today.(In this Hook opening, lasa uses the word *you* three times, there's also an appeal to the sense of taste and the

technique of somewhat mystifying the audience)

I started liking to read is when I read Jeff Kinney books. I realized that books are really enjoyable and make you laugh. I have read many books over the last 10 years, which means I have many favorite authors, such as: David Walliams, with his very popular books and, of course, Roald Dahl, with his world wide famous books. I have also disliked books like Hetty Feather. I found it quite boring. It didn't get to the problem quick enough. I also like Sky Song, as it is a fantasy and I like magical things.

In year 2, we had a day called Roald Dahl day . what we had to do was dress up as a character from a Roald Dahl book and we had to bring our very own ingredient to school and put it in a BIG (note to self)metal bowl. I could fit in that BIG bowl. I brought this liquid, including oil, which was bright red. My friend brought onions :).

At the start of year 4 to year 5, I started the Children's Book Awards and in that time I read 27 books. In the end, there was three books chosen and they were The Jam doughnut that ruined my life, The Accidental Pirates and the Eagle in The Snow. Overall, The Eagle in The Snow won. I suggest reading this book as it is very good.

Unfortunately, this is the end of my speech. I hope u liked it and didn't find it to...cheeeesy!!!(comic ending referring back to the start-bracketing technique)

Refections on Lasa's Speech

This came across as a very <u>sweet</u> speech, well structured and delivered. The sincerity of the speaker was evident as she had such an enthusiasm for the material and this conveyed itself to the audience. With her on the stage were stacks of Roald Dahl books and a Bucket and a few other props bringing the school's book day to life for the audience.

Shreya's Speech: Teachers

The imagined audience in the speech that follows is a group of six form students with the speaker is addressing their own peer group. Apparently at Shreya's school this is an annual event. Six formers are given the stage and allowed to present a satirical series of speeches. Teachers are not allowed to attend.

OMG! Hey you guys! I'm going to be talking about school and teachers today like aren't teachers just the best thing that happened to this world like aren't they just the best things (delivered with massive enthusiasm)

OMG I can't.... I just can't anymore....it's too much.(she breaks down, pauses, puts her head in her hands, then looks up and slowly says) I hate them! I hate their souls like why do they torture us what did we ever do to them?

(She puts on a rather sickly sweet Scottish accent)

"Hello girls! Good morning hope you're just having the best day!"

That's all you've seen of Mrs Clark but let me tell you, she has another side.

So, at the end of sports day, I said to MrsXXX"Mrs XXXplease can I leave I have a music lesson."

"Of course you can't Shreya what are you thinking? You have to stay here and cheer on your friends and share the school spirit!"

"But MrsXXX, I have a music lesson in 20 minutes, I have to leave now."

"Don't you dare be so rude to me young lady what are these manners???"

I bet because she likes being at school so much- I mean the woman decided to be the head of a school for god's sake- she wants everyone else to be at school all the time. I bet she has a nice old wardrobe in that big office of hers and she opens it up and out springs a double bed! That's why she's so early all the time. I bet if there was a robber at the school she would say, "OHHH PLEASE STAY WITH ME I'M SO LONELY! YOU CAN ROB THE COMPUTERS THAT WE SPENT SO MUCH MONEY ON NEXT WEEK.... PLEASE!!!"

What a loser!

Oh and don't get me started on my pastoral care teacher! Ok, you've already gotten me started. I have real respect for pastoral care teachers because they try and sort out everyone's problems and make it all la la loopsy daisy sunflower blah blah blah! But with my pastoral care teacher, I think she wants there to be a problem with people. One girl literally came in late to school and this teacher was all, "OHHHHH are you ok? Do you need financial aid? Are your parents getting a divorce?" Like no. Calm it down a bit woman! One day I was just walking down the hall and up she came and I said to her, "Mrs YYYY, something really terrible happened and I really need to talk to someone about it. I mean it's something that's really hurting me inside and out and I really feel as though it is affecting my mental health. Could I please talk to you? Pleeeeeeaaaaase?"

"Well yes of course you can talk to me about it Shreya! That's what I'm here for! Do you need tissues? You know, I basically have any kind that you want- scented, small, large, soft; anything really!"

"Well, the thing is, Mrs. YYYY, It's a papercut." (hold up finger in a lame sort of way).

"Oh Shreya! Oh Shreya, that was an awful thing to do! I can't believe you would do this to me!"

And in a way, I guess a small part of me thought that I had taught her her lesson. But I think I thought too soon because just as I am walking out of the room....

As I walk out of the room.... "So do you need financial aid? Do you need counselling? Are your parents getting a divorce?"

And that's why I love teachers!

Reflections on Shreya's Speech

This was hilarious. Shreya really went into character as she imitated the two teachers. The issue that we had in our discussions was whether or not this was more like an acting performance, a sort of stand-up comedy routine, than a public speaking exercise. We finally came to the conclusion that we could justify it as public speaking because it was based on a real public speaking event.

We had to work hard on Shreya's introduction to this piece in the exam to make this point clear. And we looked at the criterion that I always set: could this be a real speech in a real-life situation?

Arjun's Speech: VAR.

There is a reason why football is the most popular and exciting sport in the world – its simplicity. So, why do we always have to find new ways to spoil our beautiful game? (Rhetorical Question, intriguing the audience and implicitly getting the audience to agree that the game has been spoiled)

For true footballing purists, the widespread introduction of VAR this season around Europe has – from an aesthetic point of view - been an unmitigated disaster.

The natural flow and emotion in the game has been devastated due to the constant, lengthy stoppages, as incidents are reviewed. Some reviews take up to five minutes – as players and fans stand around twiddling their thumbs

This is not football. (Dramatic Pause)

Personally It takes the excitement out of football; players don't celebrate with each other after scoring a goal any more, instead they look straight towards the referee. It's removing the adrenaline and my enjoyment of football

"Football is about emotions," sniped Juventus' Sami Khedira. "Now, players don't know whether to celebrate a goal or not. That is the death of football."(Quote from an important football figure, gives weight to the case)

Lets go back to the 2014 world cup quarter final. James Rodriguez embarks on an incredible solo run from his own half, scoring one of the best overhead kicks of all time for Columbia – only for the goal to be reviewed for an eternity for a possible infringement. The referee points to a screen, which zooms into four other referees analysing another screen which lasts for an eternity.

(Hyperbole)

Can you imagine if Andres Cantor was commentating over this fixture? For those of you who don't know who Andres Cantor is, Cantor was the infamous commentator who screamed GOOOOOOAAAAAALLLLLLLL at the top of his voice after a team scores. So, Rodriguez scores a spectacular goal yet has too wait for VAR to confirm it. What would that sound like with Cantor commentating over it. GOOOAAA

checks phone, watch etc.

AAAAAAAAALLLLLLLLLLLLLL. Just like that one of the greatest goals in football had been destroyed.Rodriguez, his team-mates and millions of fans wait five minutes before celebrating while exuberant commentators withhold their comments – the emotion of the greatest goal in history has been destroyed.

But most refereeing decisions are subjective and down to human judgement.

To be truly impartial to both sides, a referee would have to review all questionable incidents or there is the risk that blatant mistakes. However, to review every incident would prompt even more soul-sapping delays. A pole going around the Bundesliga claims that professional players are saying Var has ruined the game with over 60% against the technology.

Now I prepare a toast, for the great goals in history, for the magic within the sport, to purer and more heartfelt matches, to the beautiful game.

Reflections on Arjun's Speech

This was a speech which Arjun sincerely believed in. He is passionate about a whole variety of sports and so this was the perfect subject for him his sincerity and conviction were evident throughout. He delivered a speech as if you were standing at the dinner table at a posh dinner with people who shared his passion for the beautiful game.

Ram's Speech: Water

(Before the speech had apparently started, he took a plastic water bottle from his pocket, and asked the examiner if it was ok to take a quick drink. He started to pour himself some but deliberately spilled it on the floor.Then he went straight into the following)

Water! water every where and always a drop to drink. (Pause) Well at least in the developed world that is. Now what would you do if you spilt a glass of water. Simple question really. Most of us would clean the glass of water up and probably get our selves a new one but this would be a catastrophe in the undeveloped world.

My pen friend in southern Africa wrote to me about her daily life and let me tell you know that some of the things that I heard er he then would walk back and that would be his families water supply for the rest of the day. The water that he has brought back carries thousands and thousands of bacteria from who knows where? It is said that one child dies every were shocking. Now just imagine an 8-year-old boy walking a mile on end to fetch a gallon of water. After fetching the watminute because of dirty water. Let me just let that sink in. One child dies every minute because of dirty water.(Pathos, anecdote)

My name is ram parcha and I work for a company called water aid(Introduction and Credentials). In my company we like to go around to different areas of the world and help out with any water issue that they have as we feel that clean running water is essential for everyone. We have two solutions to help out with this problem. The less severe issue and the more severe issue.

ll well mechanism that we provide to the people and wooola you have your self clean running water. We also make sure to teach the towns people how to fix it.

For the more severe problem we do the same thing and dig 16 feet into the ground but we keep a small filtration net at the bottom to make sure that any substances that could be killing the towns people are filtered out. We have another piece of equipment that is a lever and this dispenses the water. We yet again teach the towns people how to fix this.

This is whaThe less severe issue contains a few pieces of equipment and is really easy to do. We like to dig 16 feet into the ground to find our fresh water supply. Here we provide a smat we do to save the world but what can you do? (Engaging the audience)Well start your own organization, (call to action)tackle another world problem, and make the place we live in a better place or simply donate to our company. We are always grateful for any donation we get and it all goes to our trust fund to help stop this worldwide problem. We also like to take 5 lucky winners on a trip an undeveloped country with all expenses free and they can watch what we do and how we do it.

(Prop) Ahhhh that reminds about a letter that I received yesterday. I had a pen friend 3 years ago. A woman from southern Sudan anout but I realized it was talking about her village and how it had thrived soo much from when I last visited. But what surprised me the most was the fact that it wasn't the woman who wrote to me but the child !

We hope to fill these channels with water. This water will channel hope into their lives. d she told me about how her 2 month old baby was seriously ill just because of dirty water. I straightaway went out with a team and solved this severe water problem. Now you are probably wondering what this all has to do with a letter. Well it took me some time to figure (Chiasmus finish)

Reflections on Ram's Speech

Ram always likes to start his speeches in dramatic style. And, as I've said in earlier in the book, there can be a risk that a hook will be too much of a surprise. The risk here was that the examiner might think he had genuinely accidentally spilt water and would try to help. Luckily he didn't and the speech got off to a flying start.

Nice chiasmus to finish too.

Nithil's Speech: The Way we Die

Let's talk about dying. <u>(Grabs our attention)</u> We'll begin at the end.

Here is a footnote for your life: It WILL End. (Striking word play)

But what worries most people isn't the fear of being dead- rather the dying, suffering and uncertainty associated with it. Some of the suffering that we experience is important- it helps us mature, overcome and appreciate forces larger than ourselves.

But a lot of it is <u>unnecessary</u>, it serves no good purpose. It is the result of treatment often being fixated on solving the problem and forgetting there is a human being behind the diagnosis.

"Do no harm" (a quote to reinforce the point) teaches doctors to help their patients as much as they can by recommending treatment for which the potential benefits outweigh the risks of harm. This is ethical practise. It's a reminder that doctors should neither overestimate their capacity to heal, nor underestimate

306

their capacity to cause harm. (all good, logical stuff before moving on to the more controversial) And this should also be taught to people and families when they think about how they want to die and whether staying alive is just prolonging this unnecessary suffering.

Sometimes aggressive interventions are driven by a family that wants 'everything' done in innocence. They have no idea how terrible and dehumanising the process of postponing death can be. Now this is unethical practise. What matters in the end is alleviating suffering and granting the comfort and respect the person deserves.

The most important questions we should ask ourselves and encourage patients and their families to ask themselves:

1. What are your fears and worries of your condition -for the future?

2. What would be your goals if your health/condition worsens? What are your priorities?

3. What outcomes are unacceptable for you?

(Three rhetorical questions posing as a statement)

This applies to many patients in palliative care- today I wanted to tell you about a few of them. This is Kate-(shows a picture)she was diagnosed with terminal breast cancer five years ago yet just wants to know that her dog Austin is lying next to her nuzzling against her dry skin. Or take Janette-(picture)she finds it harder to breathe everyday due to Motor Neuron Disease. Well guess what?

She wants to start smoking again.

Not out of some self-destructive bent, but to feel her lungs filled while she still has them.

(A kind of rule of three thing, going on here. She has given us two examples, now the climactic, the most drama)And this is my grandad, I call him thatha. He passed away from lung cancer last year. But when he was still alive he always

said that the worst part was not being able to do anything for himself. This was the unacceptable outcome for him. He saw something so embarrassing in needing help to go to the bathroom or being spoon-fed at meals. Our priorities had changed and so did his- some days he just wanted to know what the weather was like and whilst the weather stayed pleasant, my grandad was getting worse. (Pathetic - in the rhetorical sense - story)

We thought we were doing what he wanted by continuing treatment- but he hated hospitals. The floodlit rooms lined with tubes and blinking lights and beeping machines that don't stop even when the patient's life does. Really all we can we hope for in those walls is numbness- anaesthetic. We ask too much of our hospitals. They are places for acute trauma and treatable illness- they're no place to live and die. That's not what they were designed for.

My grandad just desired comfort and respect and to feel unburdening to us.

It seems the only burden on us was being mortal.

We wanted more time with him but the truth is: more longevity means more old age not more youth. We can't prevent death... I know some of you are working on this :) but we can deal with it (pause) Honestly.

We can't wish for more time than we're capable of but we can learn to value the time we have.

And then maybe we can live well- not in spite of death, but because of it.

Reflections on Nithil's Speech

A couple of years ago I hired a local theatre and got all of my students to present their speeches to an invited audience. We added spice to it by having adjudicators and giving prizes. This speech was the overall winner. I think it was the mix of the three elements of rhetoric combined with Nithil's delivery, which was measured and clear, that did it.

In terms of the three pillars of rhetoric, you had logos with the intelligently constructed argument, pathos with the stories and ethos with the speaker establishing her personal commitment to values of empathy and caring.

Mahita's Speech: Integration

Picture yourself **(phrases like this are good because you are inviting the audience to share your vision, and by implication, all that follows)** *immigrating to another country thousands of miles away from home and stepping out of your comfort zone and take a deep breath as you prepare yourself for a new adventure and explore new land.*

*The language spoken in this country that you migrate to is completely different from your mother tongue and you only know a few basic phrases. You panic.***(this is telling you how you would behave and so, again, leading you to accept the**

speaker's case)How do I get home? Where's the local hospital? Are the police here corrupt? What are the locals like, are they nice? What do I do if my car breaks down?

Luckily for you, a couple of days later you encounter a couple of other people who come from the same place as you and speak your language. They have lived in this new country, so they can give you advice to ease the stress of moving. Naturally, you will find some common ground and form a relationship of some sort as you find it easier to communicate with than the locals.

So, you may move to the area in which they reside to stay close to them, so you can get some help easily when in need. A year or so later, another couple from your home country migrate and the process repeats itself until a small community of cognate individuals develops in this other country. You feel no need to communicate as much with the locals as this small community which has been developed provides everything that you may require in the short term. Initially, you may have moved to learn more or what not.

However, instead of grasping the given opportunity you understandably and subconsciously you continue with your life as it used to be. There are no changes whatsoever. You have not learned much about the local culture and you may have potentially squandered the chance to enrich your life. So, even though you and I; we do mix with other communities and other colours all the time but it's undeniable that we do retain network.

What I am trying to tell you **(a sort of discourse marker)** is that we subconsciously construct artificial barriers which prevent us from fully embracing all that the world has to offer and potentially breed hatred by accidentally offending certain aspects of one's culture due to a lack of understanding. Furthermore, we fear the unknown and this makes us act in irrational ways.

Now as far as solutions concerned, we clearly haven't got there yet. Other countries have tried busing and housing policies which are good, but they are heavily flawed and it's difficult to deal with these issues as they're sensitive and therefore have controversies surrounding it. I can't give a solution right here, right now but I believe that the solution lies in schools.

In my opinion, the best way to approach this situation is to implement policies which focus on our education system as we develop crucial skills in our childhood which significantly impact and play a pivotal role in our attitude towards subjects in our adulthood. Therefore, it is the ideal time as children are naturally more impressionable and open to such change.

I must stress that ethnically homogenous areas are not bad as they play an important part in preserving beautiful cultures. However, if we do not take some action we could drift into a realm of self-segregation and we could cause a violent backlash against social engineering and the progress we have made as a society other the *past century or so and inevitably prevent ourselves from becoming more aware and enriching our livelihood.*

Picture a world **(this is a reflection of the opening of the speech, we have been taken on a journey of imagination)** *in which all cultures interact. Picture a world in which the number of hate crimes has significantly decreased. Picture a world in which we don't have to constantly live in fear. This is my utopia and I hope you all can agree that it is truly beautiful.* **(Here we have the devices of anaphora and sunlit uplands.)**

Reflections on Mahita's Speech

A thoughtful and well constructed speech on an important topic. Mahita handles a sensitive issue deftly and persuasively. She invites us to imagine ourselves in a situation, explaining what our

understandable reactions to it would be and
then she extrapolates from that an
explanation of society's current situation.

Why this isn't like any old book.

First can I just say well done if you've read this far without skipping too much.

You are someone who is serious about this. You are someone people will listen to and be impressed by when you make a speech.

No question about that.

What makes this book different is that you can interact with it and make contributions.

The nature of modern publishing means I can update the book at short notice, and I will. Every three months.

Teachers.

I will particularly welcome comments from Speech and Drama Teachers and English Teachers. Have I missed out anything important? Could something have been better explained?

Students.

I'd love to hear from you guys, too. Especially if you want to try to get one of the little prizes on offer. If you send **anything** that I can use in the update, like a nice chiasmus or a good mnemonic of your own, you will get a prize and a mention. You can send anything original, that you have written yourself. When you send the email, tell me in a few sentences (not too much, I haven't got all day, about 300 words should be enough) how you think the piece could be used in a speech.

Tell me what prize you would like.

The prize isn't, like, a holiday in DisneyLand, but it will be nice.

It will be an Amazon voucher (£30 for the three that go in the book) or Chocolates or Flowers.

I'll let you choose. I'm guessing not too many flowers, right?

So the first three that I choose will go in the book and other good ones will go on my web-site. No prizes for going on the website but it may be the first step in the road to international fame. I'm not promising that. You have to be eighteen or under to enter the students' competition.

<u>www.Or8.co.uk</u>

If you are under 16 you must get your parent/guardian or carer to send it on your behalf. You must leave a phone number with your entry and this must be the number of your parent/guardian or carer.

Everyone.

Please leave a review on Amazon. This is amazingly important in helping to get the word out. Thanks.

mike@or8.co.uk

I hope you liked my book.

Seb thought it was an eye opener.

My Next Book,

How to Nail Rhetoric

A Guide for Leaders

Will be available by December 2020

A special focus on the treasure trove that is Rhetoric, this will make meetings effective, negations loaded in your favour and your presentations fantastic!

Rhetoric is the art of persuasive speaking, in the broadest sense and is an invaluable tool for those who would lead.

If you would like to know more or reserve a copy, email me:

mike@or8.co.uk

Or8

The Spoken Word

mike@or8.co.uk

Printed in Great Britain
by Amazon

43414580R00194